SAP

How to Write a
Report
Functional
Specification

SAP

How to Write a
Report
Functional
Specification

A Consultant's Guide to the secrets of
effective functional spec writing including
examples and a downloadable template

Linda R. Timms

authorHOUSE®

AuthorHouse™
1663 Liberty Drive
Bloomington, IN 47403
www.authorhouse.com
Phone: 1-800-839-8640

Published by AuthorHouse   05/14/2012

ISBN: 978-1-4685-7793-8 (sc)
ISBN: 978-1-4685-7794-5 (hc)
ISBN: 978-1-4685-7795-2 (e)

Bulk Sales

We can offer excellent discounts on this book when ordered in quantity for bulk purchases or special sales. For more information, please contact:

Sales@SAPGUIDE.CO.UK

CONTENTS

Need a Report Functional Specification template

RIGHT NOW?

Go to WWW.SAPGUIDE.CO.UK

- Click on the Templates tab to register and download your FREE Microsoft Word 2003 Report Functional Specification template

- Order your copies of the other Consultant's Guide books in the SAP range.

About the Author

After university, Linda Timms began her career learning the importance of customer service and professionalism in the banking industry, before moving into the IT field as a Business Analyst for a large telecommunications company in New Zealand. Following many years of gathering user requirements and documenting the 'inputs—processes—outputs' in various IT departments, she trained in SAP R/3 and became a 'Functional Consultant' for Ernst and Young New Zealand.

Over her successful 16 year SAP career, she has worked on implementations in Singapore, Australia and New Zealand, before taking the plunge and contracting independently in Europe and Asia. She has had the great privilege of working on SAP with a number of the main consulting firms—Price Waterhouse Consulting, IBM, Cap Gemini, Anderson Consulting, Accenture, HCL Axon, and Deloitte Consulting.

Linda Timms has become passionate about keeping up high standards in SAP implementations. Through her business consulting skills courses, she encourages attendees into striving to achieve them. Feeling it is now time to reach a wider audience, she has temporarily left the hustle and bustle of London life and moved to a sunny island in the North Atlantic Ocean to concentrate on her writing. This is the first in a series of four Consultant's Guide books that she believes will help you produce effective functional specifications, test efficiently, make a name for yourself as a top SAP consultant and be proud of what you are doing.

Acknowledgements

This book would never exist today without my many years of learning, followed by many years of trying to impart that knowledge informally and with varying success. My apologies to those that need them for harsh specification reviews and my occasional sharp tongue! I have always recognised excellent resources and was hardest on you to bring you to your full potential as SAP consultants.

We Want to Hear From You

As the reader of this book, you are the most important critic and commentator. You can email me directly to let me know what you did or didn't like about this book, as well as what you think I can do to make these books stronger.

Email: mail@SAPGUIDE.CO.UK

Please note that although I cannot help you with writing your specific functional specifications, I am available for corporate hire for coaching, seminars, and mentoring programs. Refer to my Services page at WWW.SAPGUIDE.CO.UK for more details.

Introduction

I've written this book with consultants in mind. Whether your job title is functional analyst, support analyst, IT guru, business consultant, functional consultant or something else entirely, if you are responsible for documenting or reviewing user requirements and the design approved to close that gap, then this book is for you.

The examples used are often within Sales and Distribution or Logistics processes but that is just my preference. The principles and guidelines apply across all modules, whether you are writing a report for FI CO, Plant Maintenance, or one of the many other modules within SAP.

Over the years, I have had the pleasure of working with some first-rate functional consultants who know how to draft an excellent functional specification document in a timely manner. This really helps to move a project along in the right direction, on schedule, and within budget. Likewise, I have had the not-so-pleasant task of working with not-so-first-rate functional consultants, who race through and draft functional specification documents that are not clear, inaccurate, and incomplete. Ultimately, that can result in project delays and cost overruns.

The aim of my book is to help you understand what to fill in, how and why so that you produce detailed, concise, understandable functional specs, ON TIME!

How to Use This Book

There are several ways to go through this book, and the best way for you depends on your situation.

If you are new to writing functional specifications, then I will try to make the task a little less daunting. I would suggest you start at Part 1 Essential Concepts and work your way through from there.

If you already understand the basics of a good quality functional specification and want to get to the specifics of what should go where in your document, go straight to Part 2 Specific Sections and refer to Part 3 Examples.

Don't forget, I've provided a Microsoft Word 2003 template of the Report Functional Specification on our website—the same template that I have used in the examples in this book. Just go to WWW.SAPGUIDE.CO.UK/templates and register to download your copy.

Jargon

Report Functional specification—I will refer to this in various forms throughout the book, such as functional specification, functional spec, or even just as a spec.

Functional Consultant—Your job title may differ, or your project structure might be completely unique, so wherever I use the term 'functional consultant', think functional analyst, consultant, business consultant, senior consultant, Subject Matter Expert or whatever title you are most comfortable with. I'll be referring to this role as the author of the functional spec.

Legacy System—In most of my past projects, we were helping the client move from some sort of existing system to the integrated SAP R/3 system. This 'existing system' might have been a number of small databases, or one particular database, or perhaps a combination of a database and a number of Excel spreadsheets and manual processes! Regardless of what the client used for their system before implementing SAP, for ease of use I refer to that 'system' as the legacy system.

Test Requirements—A list of key aspects and functionality that must be unit tested successfully. These aspects will be grouped logically and then turned into test cases within a test plan per group of requirements.

RIEF—Reports, interfaces, enhancements and forms! This book will only cover report functional specs.

Deploy vs Implementation—People use different terms for ultimately the same activity. That is, taking this new report 'live' in SAP. So whether your project calls the responsible person or team Deploy, Cutover, Implementation, Go Live, or the A Team, when I use deploy or implementation in my book, you will know who I am referring to!

Examples

I've included examples of report functional specs rather than SAP screenshots as each functional requirement is going to be unique. The examples have been chosen because they help illustrate a point being made in the text of the chapter, or to show you some good examples of functional spec sections that I have come across in the past, as per Part 3 of the book.

Don't worry about what version of SAP you are using or which module your requirement is within. The principles and standards outlined in this book are relevant across all SAP modules and versions.

When you download the report functional spec template, it may appear 'familiar' to you if you have previously worked with any of the main management consulting firms. Not surprisingly, there is a common theme throughout the industry on what is required in an effective functional spec! My template is similar in a lot of ways to the templates being used by these companies, although I have adapted mine to incorporate all of the better features that I have come across in functional specs over the years.

Special Highlighted Elements

Okay, so writing a functional specification is daunting and not a lot of fun for most people! I've tried to break the book up by using the following icons and texts to bring your attention to the really important bits:

*   *   * ***TOP TIP*** *   *   * Tips and tricks to save you precious time are set aside so you can spot them quickly, along with crucial information you should try and remember!

 Coffee Break sections give you a chance to take a quick break and read about some real life examples

 Alarm clock—when there is something you need to watch out for or ask about

 Cross Reference—to other topics like unit testing etc

PART 1

Essential Concepts

Chapter One

What is a functional specification?

A functional specification describes the basic functions of a software application, in this case, SAP. It is generally developed as part of the requirements analysis and acts as a blueprint for the programmers who will develop source code to meet those requirements.

Often, there are many different parties involved in the requirements analysis for each functional spec. These include the business people expected to use the end result, the functional consultants, programmers and other technical staff. The business people explain to the functional consultants exactly (well, in an ideal world), what they expect the report to do, from a business perspective.

The business requirements are then merged with other data that needs to be captured, and is used to help clarify the way the report will function. All of this analysis must be completed in order to document the functional specification.

This book is about *functional specifications*, not *technical* specifications. My functional specification template includes a Technical Specification section because I think it's important to have the whole solution documented in one place. So in Part 2 Specific Sections, I will give a brief overview of what goes into that section but the focus of this book is the functional side, not the technical. To me, the key difference between a functional specification and a technical specification is your perspective.

1. A *functional specification* describes how the system will work entirely from the **user's perspective**. It doesn't care how the thing is coded. It talks about features. It lists the key aspects that must be included. It specifies screens, menus, outputs, and so on. It describes how the report will be used, when and why.

2. A *technical specification* describes the internal implementation of the program. It talks about data structures, relational database models, coding used etc.

When you design SAP functionality, the most important thing is to pin down the user experience. For a report, that means understanding what the user needs on selection screens, how the report will be run and when, what it will be used for and what the output is going to be.

*   *   * TOP TIP *   *   *

The functional spec should always reflect the latest design and be a complete resource of what was designed, why and how it was achieved.

*   *   *

 For other SAP functionality like interfaces, enhancements and forms, there will be a whole set of different user requirements to take into consideration. I cover the specific sections for those in other books within The Consultant's Guide series.

Chapter Two

Why is it important?

And where does it fit in the Big Picture?

Now I bet you thought that once you had written your draft functional spec and pushed it through the review and sign off process, that would be it. Right? Wrong! Although a functional spec might be identified and approved in the design phase, as soon as it gets to unit testing, you can start to need some changes and tweaks. Perhaps during unit testing, you notice one of the key features cannot be triggered in the way you had intended. Maybe your ABAP Developer has had to shorten selection field names or column headings due to space constraints. Then, throughout the testing cycles, you are likely to have changes (hopefully small) that need to be reflected in the functional spec.

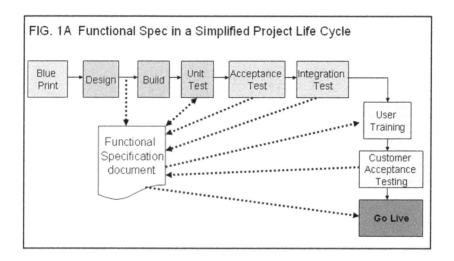

FIG. 1A Functional Spec in a Simplified Project Life Cycle

Even after successful testing, your functional spec is an important document. The Training team will refer to it (and probably you as the author), to understand the design so that they can prepare their training materials appropriately.

When the end users finally get to test the report for themselves, they might decide that some key features have been missed, requiring someone to go back to your functional spec to check the original requirements requested. Perhaps performance is an issue when it's run with a lot of historical transactional data, requiring a change to the original technical design. All these changes will follow your project's standard change control procedure but if they are approved, then the functional spec should be updated accordingly to reflect what the end design will be.

It's not over then, though! As author of the functional spec, your immediate responsibilities may have finished with the signed off and tested report. But to be thorough and professional, you want this report to Go Live successfully, don't you? I always include a 'Deploy' section in my functional spec for how to take the report live.

- Do the folks involved in Go Live support need to set up any variants or background jobs?

- Is it reliant on specific master or transactional data to run successfully?

- Are there custom table entries to be maintained?

- Do the users running the report in Production need special authorisations?

*   *   *TOP TIP*   *   *

The best time to think and capture all of these pieces of key information is during the initial writing of the functional spec. As the author, you are the one asking the questions and collecting all of the details for the report at your fingertips.

*   *   *

Your Functional Spec is going to be:

- The basis for technical design

- The basis for what needs to be unit tested and how

- Provide input into which relevant scenarios (business processes) should be included into the business Acceptance testing

- Provide input into which cross functional processes will be impacted for the scoping of Integration testing

- Act as the basis for end customer signoff—does it meet their original requirements?

- Provide the key information for Go Live preparation and Cutover activities, Training preparation, and Post Go Live Support

Remember, it should always reflect the latest design.

So, no pressure then!

Chapter Three

Who will use it and How?

Specs can be thorough and complete, but are not of any use if nobody reads them. You want your spec to be accurate and up-to-date, but also easily understood by the numerous people, job roles, and teams that are going to refer to it at various points in the project life cycle.

Let's take a look at who they are and why they are interested in your design:

Peer reviews—I'll talk about this in more detail in Chapter Seven. Your functional spec is going to have to be read and approved by multiple people. Often a more senior consultant or team lead will do an 'internal team' quality check on it. They will be looking to see that the design is appropriate, the various sections of the functional spec are complete and that the spec is of a good enough standard to pass the next level of quality checks. No-one wants to let shoddy work through to the next level and then get blamed for not doing their job properly!

Sometimes when the consultant writing the spec is based offshore, an onshore consultant is assigned to review the spec before it is approved for the Design Authority or Architect to give the final sign off. Again, in addition to checking the content of the functional spec, the onshore consultant needs to make sure they point out any gaping holes in the information presented, ensuring that the design meets the requirements originally identified.

Design Authority / Architect / Program Manager—Depending on the size of your project team, you will have one or more of all of these roles represented! This is the person or people that have the final say on whether your design is the right one to meet the user requirements, whether it's been described in sufficient and clear detail and so on. If you have gotten it wrong, it's this person that will take the brunt of it if they don't pick up on the misunderstandings or errors when reviewing the spec.

Security Team—Those wonderful people who create job roles and assign authorizations and restrictions to user ID's will probably be interested in your spec if you have defined a new transaction code to run the new report. They may only read the 'Overview' section and the relevant section in the spec that describes the security aspects, but often the Technical Build Team cannot begin without having a sign off by the Security team first.

*   *   * TOP TIP *   *   *

If you are lucky enough to be working in a small project team without such rigid sign off processes, when you write the security section of your functional spec, take ten minutes to run it past someone in the Security team. You can do this either in person or by email, just to make sure they are aware of it and that you have included the details that they need to make it happen. They usually appreciate the 'heads up' and will be more inclined to help you out with testing roles for the various environments when you need them!

*   *   *

Technical Team—This is a small heading for what could be a number of people wanting to understand what is in your spec! During the spec writing phase, you may have already spoken to someone in the ABAP development team to check your ideas or help you prototype if it is something very different or complicated. If not, the first time the technical team have seen the detail of your design will be when you send them a copy of your spec. They will be checking to make sure it's understandable, complete, and includes sample data and process steps for them to use in their build and initial testing stages.

Other Functional Teams—If your report is solely for use within the Finance Team for instance, then your spec may not be of interest to other teams working on other modules. But if for example it retrieves sales data for reporting with Accounts Receivable information, you may want to bring it to the attention of the Sales and Distribution Team and ask them to have a quick read through of what you have designed.

I have often found that making the other teams aware of my design that might impact on their areas was very useful for flushing out any incorrect assumptions on my part, or streamlining the design because I wasn't fully aware of the functionality available in those other teams and they were. So think through any integration points with other modules and pass your spec to them once your design has been drafted to see if they can highlight any potential issues or make suggestions for improved design.

*   *   * TOP TIP *   *   *

A good Consultant is constantly improving and not afraid to ask for input or feedback.

*   *   *

*   *   *   *   *   *

Previously, I worked on a very large project team within the Distribution team. There was a separate team responsible for 'Sales' that took care of everything from enquiries and contracts through to sales order processing, and then the subsequent billing functions. Another team looked after the Logistics Supply Chain functions, such as warehouse activities, materials management and stock planning. Our Distribution team were responsible for the deliveries and transportation shipment processes, whether they were from a Sales process, or a Supply Chain process. It was a busy project and as consultants, we only had time to be aware of the design in our own specific team.

One day, I received an email from a junior consultant in the Logistics Supply Chain team with his draft functional spec attached, asking me to have a quick read through and let him know if it impacted on our Distribution design in any way.

From his Overview and process flow model, I could see that he had a business requirement for a month end report to analyse certain stock movements. His detailed design was proposing to capture specific information into a custom table, using the user exit at Post Goods issue of an outbound delivery. On first reading, that sounded okay and his own Peer Review had agreed the design but thankfully this consultant was brave enough to ask for our team's feedback! Had he gone ahead with his design, we would probably only have noticed during Acceptance testing when his user exit slowed the goods issue of our 5,000 deliveries a day to a standstill!

As his report requirement was for a month end timeframe, it was not critical that his custom table be updated the very instant that a delivery was goods issued, and given the volume of transactions being processed, his initial design would have caused us terrible performance problems! Instead, we were able to talk him through some alternative designs that wouldn't impact performance. He settled on using a background job that ran nightly to pull the relevant goods movements from the Material Document table MSEG and update his custom table accordingly.

It only took an hour or two for us to review his design and make the alternative suggestions, and required only a little re-work on his part since the Technical Team had not yet started development. A whole lot less re-work than what would have been required if he had not brought it to our attention during his Review process!

*   *   *

Key Business Resource—Often the original requirements are sponsored by a particular business area or resource. I've found it really useful to schedule a short review of my design with that business resource BEFORE I push the spec through for final signoff. This is sometimes easier to do than others, I admit!

If a business contact has been named as 'owning' the user requirements, then I try to have a ten minute conversation (or online conference if face to face is impossible) with them to run them through my design in a high level. I don't mean talking them through the spec word by word. Most of the detail in the spec isn't relevant for them. What they want to know is that I have understood their requirements, that I understand how the report is to be used by the business, and that the report they will end up with meets those requirements.

I concentrate on the overview. I list for them which business processes I think are relevant and ask if I have missed any, and I explain at a high level how I see the report will be run, how often, and what the output will look like. Obviously I can't show them anything in SAP yet but I will probably have a PowerPoint mock up showing the columns and contents, selection screen and so on. If I've gotten something glaringly wrong or I have missed something out completely, this review will let me know. It is more direct than just sending them a copy of the functional spec and hoping that they read it, assuming 'no response' is acceptance of it!

*   *   * TOP TIP *   *   *

If you feel uncomfortable about doing this kind of review with your Business Process Owner or maybe that it is not your position to contact the business resource in this way, suggest it to your Team Lead or the Design Authority. Explain how you see it could be very beneficial in the long run to get this informal 'okay' of the design now, before the Technical team begin developing it.

*   *   *

Training Team—As mentioned in Chapter Two, when you design a new report, someone will have to figure out how to train the end users who might have to run it, monitor it, or use its output. They often won't become aware of its existence until well into the testing phases, long after you have moved onto writing your next specs!

If you've done a good job of making your spec understandable and describing how it will be run and so on, then the Training Team can make a start by reading your spec.

If your spec is complicated or hard to follow, they will probably give up and just come and demand your time to go through it with them in detail, most likely at a time when you are very busy working on something completely different.

*   *   ** TOP TIP **   *   *

It's in your best interests to put the effort in when you are writing your spec to save yourself time and repeated effort later on! It will also make you stand out as a 'good' consultant and your reputation for producing good quality professional work will grow!

*   *   *

Go Live / Cutover / Deploy Team—On smaller projects, I've been involved in the design, build, test and then deployment of the functionality in my functional specs. That is great when it happens as you get that feeling of satisfaction to see something you've created going all the way to being used in a live environment.

But sometimes that isn't the case. Maybe you have changed roles within the project team, or moved onto another project team altogether before your report goes live. Or maybe there are teams of people whose responsibilities are very specific to just this part of the project life cycle. If this is the case, or indeed if there is a chance you may not be around to push this new report live yourself, then you need to ensure that the relevant and critical pieces of information for those activities are summarized in your functional spec.

*   *   **TOP TIP**   *   *

At a glance, I should be able to pick up your spec and understand from the overview what the report is and how its used, and then from the deploy section, what pre-requisites I need to have in place for the end users to successfully use this report in future.

*   *   *

Chapter Four

Where is the information that I need?

The content of a functional spec must be tuned to the flavour of the RIEF object that it is describing. Since they perform very different tasks, a report specification document should be very different from an interface, enhancement, or form functional spec. Using functional specification templates helps to ensure the appropriate content for each type of RIEF object.

Larger project teams will provide you with their own functional spec formats to be used, often following the specific methodology in place. Other projects will not have any formal documentation procedures at all and it may be up to you to determine what will go in your spec and what won't.

The trouble with using any template is that it scares people away from writing the spec because it looks like such a daunting task. But I am a fan of using templates. Why?

- I don't want to have to remember all the various types of information that I know should be in a spec for a well-designed report. My memory just isn't that good any more!

- I can have hints and tips included as 'hidden text' in my templates to remind me what a section or title in the spec means. Particularly useful if I only write report functional specs every now and then.

- My specs are formatted clearly and consistently which makes them a lot easier to read and follow.

- My work is more professional. Because I am familiar with my own templates, when I am taking a business user through my design, showing a trainer or explaining what I want to an ABAP developer, I know where the relevant pieces of information are in the document and can flick to it with ease.

- At a glance of the functional spec table of contents, I can remind myself of the types of information that I need to gather and the questions I need to ask before I can begin writing.

If your project team has its own methodology and template for documentation, then you will need to use that. Some sections may be common to those in my templates. The template that I use (REPORT_FS.doc) and that you can download from our website (WWW.SAPGUIDE.CO.UK) is large and 'thorough'!

If you are on a small project where documentation is not policed with vigour, you could get away with a simpler version (BASIC_FS.doc), or come up with your own.

Regardless which format you use, make sure you document clearly and concisely the user requirements and how your design meets them, using the principles, tips and tricks I document in this book!

Having determined what format your functional spec is going to take, you now need to figure out what information you have already got, and what information you are going to need to complete the spec.

Like every good consultant, try to think about it from an Inputs—Processes—Outputs point of view.

Inputs—Think about the origin of the functional spec you have been asked to write

- Where has the user requirement come from?

- Have I been given a high level design document?

- Are the requirements documented in a change request or a series of emails?

- Are there additional notes from meetings on the topic?

- Who else has been involved in discussing the user requirement so far—another consultant? The architect?

Basically, I want to **gather all the possible background information on the user requirement**, not just what I've been handed which is often just a two line description!

Processes—Having a look at the sections in the functional spec template you are going to use, you can start writing a list of questions that you need answers to.

For instance,

- What business area has requested the report?

- What type of information will it report?

- Which areas of the business will be running the report?

- Is it a brand new requirement or a replacement of a report currently available in a legacy system? If it's a replacement, I will need full details (preferably the old spec!) of the current report so I can see the types of information and levels of detail to be included.

- When will it be run and how often?

Outputs—More questions to be answered:

- What volume of data are we expecting it to trawl through and output?

- Do we know the preferred output format? That is, what is it going to look like, what information should be included, what method of execution?

- What area of the business should be advised if the report fails (and how should they be advised!)

And so on . . . .!

Chances are whoever has handed the requirement to you to write the spec will not have all the answers! But as soon as you can, get your list of questions together and then find out who can answer them. Often the Design Authority or Architect will know a bit more detail, and it will be up to you to determine what the best answer is for some of them. And sometimes it will mean finding a key business resource to give you some of the answers.

In Part 2 of this book, I will work through the sections of my report functional spec template and try to highlight the key questions that need to be answered in that particular section by using this 'alarm clock' icon.

* * *TOP TIP* * *

A word of warning about relying on High Level Design (HLD's) documents!

In some projects, one consultant (often based onshore with the main project team) will be asked to prepare a high level design document for the new report and pass that to a second consultant (often based in an offshore resource team) to complete the functional spec, based on that design. The HLD will be a summary of the functional spec with some headings being the same and others not being mentioned at all.

Project Management like this approach because to them it means the more expensive and experienced onshore resources are only involved in giving a clear direction to the more plentiful and less expensive offshore resources. The total cost of development for the new report is therefore going to be less overall. Unfortunately, use of an HLD doesn't always get the results that management would like!

Let's look at it from the Onshore Consultant's point of view first:

He's been involved in some meetings about this new report and understands what is required. He is looking forward to getting his teeth into it and doing a really good job! Then he is told that he needs to limit his input to just an HLD, and pass his knowledge over to the offshore consultant who will complete the functional spec (and take all the credit for it)! He will have the not so fun task of reviewing it, maybe a couple of times, before passing it on to the Design Lead for sign off. Perhaps he feels he is better experienced or more knowledgeable than the consultant he is passing over to, and that he could do the whole functional spec himself quicker and better than anyone else could!

The common result is that he will put too much detail into the HLD to compensate for not being allowed to write the functional spec himself and put his 'stamp' of design all over it. The risk with this is that it will appear almost complete and the offshore consultant may not bother with thinking for himself or questioning any part of it.

From the Offshore Consultant's point of view:

He's been tasked with finishing off seven integration process tests, writing the unit test for a new enhancement, and now he is told by his team lead that he must join a knowledge transfer phone call to accept this new HLD and have the functional spec written for that within two weeks!

The knowledge transfer consists of the onshore consultant going through the HLD word for word, takes up an hour of his time, and since this is the first he has heard of this new requirement, he hasn't had a chance to come up with any thoughts or suggestions on the design himself!

He can make life easy for himself (and keep his team lead off his back) by copying and pasting as much as possible from the HLD into his functional spec template. Any areas not specifically covered in the HLD, he will bluff his way through, getting the functional spec to review status as soon as possible.

Although this might seem the best option to take, if he doesn't fully understand the new requirement and the business processes that are going to use it, the design may not be the most appropriate, it will not be tested properly, and will probably require many change requests later down the project life cycle to correct it. His alternative might feel like he is wasting the first week trying to understand the requirement, asking questions and waiting for replies, and juggling all his other tasks, to end up doing a rushed job just to meet the deadlines!

If your project uses an HLD as a handover to a second consultant (for example, you), for writing the functional spec, try and improve the process and the outcomes by doing the following:

- As soon as you are made aware of the new requirement coming your way, ask for a copy of the High Level Design AND any other background information to be sent to you with enough time for you to realistically review it all BEFORE any knowledge transfer session is set up.

- After reviewing all of the information you have been sent, make up a list of questions that are still unanswered. You can use the list of questions for each section of the functional spec (see Part 2 of this book) and cross off any that you have already been given answers to.

- Send the list of questions back to the originating consultant before the knowledge transfer session, and then go through them one by one during that session. Make a note against each question of either the answer given, or who has taken responsibility for finding out the answer and by when. After the session, send your updated list with the notes by email so that everyone is aware what the next steps are.

By doing this, you are making it clear that you want and need to understand the new requirement to be able to do a good professional job on the functional spec and that you need more information than what has been provided already. If you are the originating consultant writing the HLD and handing over to someone else, try and follow these guidelines too, knowing that by doing so, you are being professional and thorough and ensuring that the best possible design and functional spec will be the outcome, regardless of who does the actual writing of it!

*   *   *

Chapter Five

When do I need to have this done by?

As soon as you know you have a functional spec to write, ask this question! Depending on the size of the project, the phase in the Life Cycle, and how many other requirements are being worked on at the same time by the same resources, you will get very varied answers.

After asking for all of the background information on the requirement, reviewing it and making up your list of questions that you need answered, you are in a better position to understand the complexity of the report required. Once you have written many functional specs, you get quicker at producing them but to begin with, you will need to allow yourself enough time to do a decent job. If your team lead is expecting you to produce the functional spec while also completing many other time consuming and critical tasks, then you will need to ask them to prioritise what comes first!

Find out how much time has been allotted for producing the functional spec and having it completely approved and signed off. Then think about the review process (see Chapter Seven).

Are the reviewers going to be available towards the end of this spec writing phase or will you need to take into account their workload or holidays? Take different time zones into consideration too.

* * * **TOP TIP** * * *

If you need answers from a resource working on a different time zone to yours, make it work in your favour. Send your request so that they will get it at the start of their day. Suggest that they send their response to you before the end of their day so that you will have it available at the start of yours!

* * *

It often takes a few days to schedule in a review of a functional spec with a very busy Design Architect, and only they will know what other commitments are against their time. So if you have three weeks to get the functional spec written and signed off, remember that your Design Architect might take a day to review it and then want some changes made before reviewing it again. You need to have your first draft ready for his or her first review at the beginning of that third week. If you have more than one level of review to get through, then you need to allow **at least a day per level** and book in the review time with them now so that you know for sure you won't be delayed because they can't fit you in at the last moment.

Okay, stop panicking and let's get started!

Chapter Six

How do I start?

This is how I tackle a new functional spec:

1. **Ask for all the relevant information and background**. This might be a change request document, a high level design, a handover session from another consultant, some emails, meeting notes and so on.

2. **Begin a list of questions** that you know will need to be answered to provide a full detailed functional spec. To do this, I go through each section in the functional spec template and remind myself the type of information I need to fill in. See Part 2 for a summary of questions per template section. Remember, some of these questions you will need to answer yourself as you work through the detailed design!

3. If any of the questions haven't been answered by the background information, **find out who will give you the answers and send them the questions**. Be firm about when and how you will follow up with them to get the answers. Explain that the functional spec is dependant on those answers, and the timeline you are working to.

4. **Start the document**! The more you can do immediately the better! So, determine the template to be used, and begin. You should have enough basic information to fill in the title page, headers and footers, document control sections and so on. You may already have the answers to some of the questions so you can write those in as well.

5. **Any questions that you need to answer are next**. For instance, if it's a replacement report from a legacy system, you will need to identify the source of each of the column contents within SAP. If it's a brand new report, you will need to decide the layout and contents, some of which may have been provided to you already.

6. **Prepare process flows and extraction logic diagrams.** If you can, sketch these roughly on paper and then see if your team lead can get someone else to turn them into Microsoft PowerPoint pictures for you. Often there will be someone in Admin or a junior in the team that has a bit more time available and can spend precious hours getting the boxes and lines drawn straight so all you will have to do is check it and make small adjustments if necessary before copying them into your spec.

Basic rules for writing a good functional spec:

- Make it understandable—start with the 'big picture' then fill in the details

- Break things down into short sentences. If you are having trouble writing a sentence clearly, break it into two or three shorter ones.

- Don't use stilted, formal language because you think it's unprofessional to write in simple sentences. Use the simplest language you can. Why use 'utilise' when 'use' is perfectly clear?

- Make sure you use real words and spell check! The number of times I have seen 'updation' in specs and even caught it coded into an enhanced screen way down the process at integration testing is scary!

- Your spec should be factual and not contain any personal opinions or words that suggest opinion such as 'I think' (you should know!) or 'Obviously' (what might be obvious to you might not be to one of the spec readers so drop words like that out completely).

- Avoid entire pages with just text. Use numbered or bulleted lists, tables, and flow charts to make the spec easier to read and understand.

- Make sure your detailed design section flows in a logical and sensible order. Think it through—would you describe the output first and then the selection screen and selection logic? No! Start with the selection screen, explain the logic required behind each of the fields, provide a mock up of it (but don't waste too much precious time here!), then proceed to the online output, and so on.

- Review and reread your spec several times. When you find a sentence that isn't super easy to understand, rewrite it.

Chapter Seven

The Review and Signoff Process

The diagram below is the sign off steps that one of my recent projects used for every functional spec. Your project team might have less review points, or maybe even more! The point is, in a worst case scenario, every single one of your review points may want you to make changes to your functional spec before they agree to sign it off to the next level!

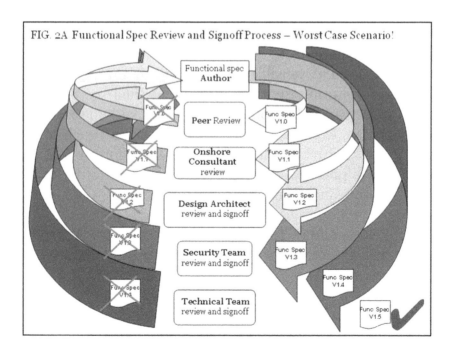

FIG. 2A Functional Spec Review and Signoff Process — Worst Case Scenario!

In this example, it's the SIXTH iteration that finally meets with everyone's approval! Can you imagine how much re-work that is, how long it takes to not only get the first round of approval from each review point, but also how much time it takes to get them to review it again and again, every time you have incorporated the additional changes wanted by one of the review levels?

Regardless of how many levels your project has for signing off a functional spec, your aim is to reduce the 'rejections' and time involved in getting your document approved by putting as much effort into your spec as humanly possible within your time constraints.

*   *   * TOP TIP *   *   *

Know your audience! In relation to getting your functional spec approved, your 'audience' are the various people and roles that are going to review your spec. Try and find out from your colleagues or your Team Lead what the key reviewers 'like' or 'dislike' in functional specs.

*   *   *

For instance, in Figure 2A, I would say the key reviewers are the onshore consultant and the Design Architect, as my 'peer review' is often done by a senior consultant in my own team who I know will give me good honest feedback and is available on the same working hours as I am.

Which onshore consultant is going to be involved in the review? Some consultants are pedantic about having every single section completed before the review starts (like me for instance!). Although some people prefer wordy descriptions to diagrams or bullet points, it's not so much about getting the format of the information right for each reviewer as that would be very difficult. Each of us comes from a slightly different mix of background and experience, and often a consultant will be particularly strict about completing a certain part of the spec in detail because that is where their own background and experience lies and so they feel it has added importance.

I've found that reviewers that have joined the project from a business role background will pay particular attention to the overview, the process flows and the testing sections as that is what they understand the most.

One particular consultant had joined our design team from a Deploy role so you can guess which part of the spec he was particularly interested in reviewing!

Other consultants in your review cycle may be from a more technical background who concentrate more on the functional solution section being clearly and logically defined.

Then other consultants will let a functional spec through their review with only minimal effort in certain parts of the spec but the Design Architect will hopefully reject it if it comes through to him or her in that state.

I don't advocate skimping on your functional spec just because you might know that the reviewers are not going to be too strict—that is lazy and unprofessional. But it does help to understand the emphasis that your reviewers are going to put on certain parts of the spec and pay particular attention to the detail in those areas to give yourself an easier review time.

Writing a really good detailed functional spec does take a lot of time and effort but it often won't involve constant 'writing' for two weeks straight. For instance, when you first determine what questions you still need answers for, it may take a few days or longer to get some of those answers back. In that time, you can be chipping away at other areas in the functional spec such as the Document Semantics section, and if you know where and how the report is going to be triggered, you can start drafting up a process flow diagram for section 4 of the spec.

*   *   * ***TOP TIP*** *   *   *

Rather than waiting until the final few days of your allotted spec writing time, why not run relevant aspects of your design past some of the reviewers informally to get their input and agreement before it requires too much re-work on your part?

I often encourage consultants to schedule in 30 minutes with the Design Architect and the responsible onshore consultant. Talk them through the solution, making sure that those who will have a say in the sign off of the design are all aligned and agreed on the solution, within the first week of spec writing. Do this even if it means showing them scribbled drawings and talking it through, rather than having slides or flow charts available which take precious time to prepare.

*   *   *

The purpose of the review process is to make sure that the functional specification documents are complete, accurate, and contain the approval signatures required to move on to the technical design phase. In some projects, a Quality Assurance Checklist is used as the basis of the review, to make sure that functional specs are consistently reaching the desired standard.

You should become familiar with the QA checklist used within your own review process. If you don't have one, then have a look at the following example so you can see the points that a good reviewer is looking for in your functional spec.

FIG. 2B RIEF Review Checklist

QA Document

Details of the RIEF

RIEF Name:	
Release:	
RIEF Version:	
RIEF Author:	
Functional Reviewer:	
Reviewer:	
Date of review:	

Area: RIEF

Item	Check	NA	OK	Not OK	Comment	Status
Doc Controls						
1.1	Appropriate use of Functional Spec template?					
1.2	Date and version control are updated?					
1.3	Amendment history along with date / Author / Description updated?					
1.4	Approvers names and roles completed?					
1.5	Business process owner identified?					
1.6	Project naming conventions followed					
Spec details						
2.1	Overview – does the overview describe what is required, by which business area, why?					
2.2	Report description, controls and dependencies are adequately defined?					
2.3	Starting conditions, volume, frequency and error handling all detailed?					
2.4	Any business unit impacted/Dependency should be clearly identified and					
2.5	Security aspects have been described clearly					
2.6	Assumptions/Exclusions – Identified clearly					
2.7	Functionality described agrees with the High Level Design? Functional solution is clearly and logically detailed? Data extraction is clear?					
2.8	Testing requirements / Data sets for Technical team and unit test / Unit test Plan has been provided					
2.9	Deploy section updated with any background jobs required, data conversion, support requirements?					
General						
3.1	General QA on Functional Spec - grammar, understandability. Avoid Short wordings (PO should be Purchase Order, BE should Business entity)					
3.2	Functional Spec saved in the correct file location, status updated accurately?					
3.3	Functional spec passed Onshore consultant review?					
3.4	All QA points recommended in the review are incorporated as part of FS modification.					
3.5	Meeting setup is done with Design Architect in advance of FS finish date?					

PART 2

Specific Sections

In Part 3, you will find the website link to the report functional spec template that I use. Below is the Table of Contents from that template and I will now take you through each of these sections and explain what I believe you should be putting into them for a really good, detailed, clear report functional spec. I have used the template numbering system with each of the sub-headings so you can follow which part of the functional spec we are looking at easier.

 Note, if you are after only a basic functional spec template, the website has one of these too with basic guidelines on how to complete it in the hidden text.

FIG. 3A Report Functional Spec Template Table of Contents

Contents

Chapter Eight

1. Document Semantics

This is an important but dull section of the functional spec as it acts as a reference for who created or changed the document and why, who 'owns' it and who approved it. Larger projects can be running for many years and an early report may have been enhanced many times, requiring additional extensions to functionality. Whichever team ends up supporting these developments in the live environment will need easy to understand, clear functional specs to aid them, including a section that clearly defines what changes were made to the report, when, and against which change request or issue.

1.1 Document Properties

In this section, you need to detail the owner and contact information. It is important that the author of the spec is noted against 'document prepared by' so that there is a single point of reference for anyone reading the spec in future should they have questions about the content. The author is responsible for making sure the spec is complete and accurate. If the original author has moved onto another project and is no longer available, the main consultant responsible for the latest change should update the author details with their own to keep it current.

Where possible, note the business owner's name and / or business area against 'Process Owner', and an email address or phone number in the 'Contact Information' box. This makes it very easy at a later stage for other teams such as Training Development to know who to contact for more in depth understanding of how this report fits into the business processes.

The 'Responsible Team' will be the SAP team or module that the author is part of and who are responsible for defining the requirements and seeing it through to completion.

1.2 Amendment History

Amendment history becomes relevant and critical once the functional spec has been approved and development is underway. From that point on, any changes to the design will need to be listed here in the 'Summary of Changes Since Last Revision' and the revision number updated accordingly. Then everyone referring to the spec knows what changes were approved, when, and in reference to which Change Request or Issue Log number.

During the drafting of the spec which can take a few attempts, and the review process which may require a fair few changes, the revision number is not so important. I will put the Revision / Version number as 1.0 and leave the 'Summary of Changes Since Last Revision' blank regardless of how many changes I have incorporated as these are only really relevant to keep record of changes AFTER the initial version is completely signed off and built. Note, the version number on the document title page should reflect the current revision number in the 'amendment history'.

1.3 Distribution

This section contains a list of the recipients of the document, what role they hold and what level of input to the spec they have. It is important to think through all the relevant parties that may need to know about the development, as well as those that will need to give sign off approval to it.

The levels of input can differ accordingly:

Recipient: Examples of recipients where no feedback or input is necessarily expected might be other project team leads where you are including them in the distribution list so that they are aware of the new report and possible impacts on them. For example, the Support Team responsible for post go-live support should be the recipient of every new functional spec so that they are aware early on in the project life cycle of new developments that they will need to support in future.

Review: Some recipients will be included solely for review purposes such as the Business Owner of the original requirement. It always pays to keep them in the loop and although a lot of the spec will be 'too technical' for them to be bothered with, you should include them in the distribution and ask them to review the 'overview' (section 3 of the template) and 'general information' (section 4 of the template) sections, in particular the 'assumptions and exclusions' so that their expectations of what they will get back for acceptance are set accurately.

Input: Often you may have another functional consultant assigned who has provided you with the high level design or perhaps assisted in pinning down the requirements. In these cases, you will want that role to review and perhaps make suggestions for input into your spec. This often happens when the 'author' is offshore, sending the spec to their onshore counterpart for review and input.

Approval: Usually you will be looking for final signoff and approval of your functional spec from a Design Architect,

Design Authority, Team Lead or Project Manager. It's once this person has given their approval that the spec will be passed to the Technical Team for review.

1.4 Approval

Some project methodologies will require the final approved functional spec to be printed off and signed for audit purposes. If this is the case, then this section should hold the name and title of each of the approvers, with space for them to put the date and their signature once printed. If your project doesn't have a requirement for this, then leave the section blank or delete it from your template.

 Key Questions:

- Who is the business process owner and how do I contact them if I have further questions on the requirements?

- Who within my own team will I need to distribute a copy of the spec to? What level of review do I expect from each? What do I know about the reviewer's background and how that may weight certain parts of the functional spec in their eyes?

- What other teams will I need to circulate a copy of the spec to?

- Who will give my spec approval? What dates for completion do I need to work towards? Will the reviewers and approvers be available around those dates or do I need to schedule in sessions with them earlier than those dates to be sure?

Chapter Nine

2. QA's and Signoffs

FIG. 4A QA's and Signoffs

Design		Tech Design		Program Unit Test		Deploy	
QA Date:		QA Date:		QA Date:		QA Date:	
Author		Author		Developer		Author	
Business Owner		Business Owner		Basis/DBA		Business Owner	
Analyst		Analyst		Analyst		Analyst	
		Developer		Business Owner		Developer	
Security		Security				Security	
Basis/DBA		Basis/DBA				Basis/DBA	
Support		Support				Support	

This table in the template is a good way of keeping track of where the Quality Assurance checks and signoffs are up to if your project doesn't have a separate method of tracking the status of the functional spec. As each reviewer approves the spec, they should add their name to the relevant box for the Design or Tech Design Column.

Once unit testing is completed by the developer, he or she should put their name in that field and the date. Once QA checks are done within the Technical team and its handed back to the author or 'analyst' for formal unit testing, the next boxes are filled in with the appropriate names.

If your project is not rigid with controls in this area or has a separate method of monitoring status and progress of the functional specs being written, then this section will not be relevant for you in which case you can leave the section blank or delete it from your template.

Chapter Ten

3. Overview

This is the all important introduction to the report. It's the one section of the functional spec that almost everyone you circulate the document to will actually read! Try and answer as many of these questions as possible, and then work the answers into a clear, factual but brief overview of the report being defined:

 Key Questions:

Who? Which business units have requested the report? Is it country specific or a global requirement? Is it just a single distribution channel within this business area or will the report have wider use? Will there be any restrictions on who can run the report and access the data? Who would need to be advised if the report fails to run and what is the preferred method of advice?

What? Summarise what the report will contain and its use. For instance, 'a report of the deliveries where the pre-printed document number has not yet been scanned by shipping point' is enough detail for the Overview. The 'Report Description' in Section 4 of the Functional Spec template will cover this in a lot more detail. Think also of what the report data contains and ask about expected volume of data.

Why? Is it a legal requirement? Is it replacing a business critical report from a legacy system? Why is the report needed? What would the impact to the business be if this report was not produced? E.g. would delays in deliveries or delays in invoicing occur? The answers to these questions will help you determine which business processes are impacted, and therefore should be included in Integration and Acceptance Testing phases which concentrate more on the end to end process rather than the specific development.

When? How often will the report be run and when? For example, is it a daily requirement or perhaps only at month end? Will multiple business user groups be running the report simultaneously?

Where? Will this report be run locally at the business units or centrally in a support area? Will it need to be automated via a background job? If the report will be run from multiple geographical locations, is there a language requirement to be considered? Where will the output be generated—to a local printer, a centralized printer, or maybe to nominated email accounts?

Remember: this section is an overview and you need to keep it as a fairly high level summary of the report while touching on each of these areas. You will be covering the detailed answers to these questions in the other sections of the spec so make sure you get the answers even though they will only be summarized in this section—brief but clear!

Chapter Eleven

4. Functional Specification Overview

Section Four of the functional spec template covers an introduction to the report at a lower level of detail than the overview. I have used the template numbering system with each of the sub-headings so you can follow which part of the functional spec we are looking at easier.

4.1 General Information

4.1.1 Business Units Impacted:

In this section, you need to state which business units will be impacted by the introduction of this new report. Have a think about the organizational structure and also where this requirement has originated from. If you are not sure whether you know all of the business areas that will need to run this report or who will receive the output for analysis, then contact your Business Process Owner (the originator of the requirement) and ask.

This information is key to determining which business processes are relevant, and therefore the transactional data that you will need to use in your Unit Testing. Later in the project cycle, this information will be used to help determine the scope of Integration Testing and Customer Acceptance

Testing. It will also help the Training Team determine which roles in which business areas are impacted by the report.

4.1.4 Scope:

Filling in the Business Units Impacted section goes hand in hand with understanding the scope of the report which also needs to be documented. Perhaps the report is intended to only cover certain types of product or customers of a certain classification? Maybe only specific sales areas or distribution channels will be in scope? Is it only to include deliveries that have been 'post goods issued' in the past 7 days; or transportation shipments that have reached a certain status? You will need to be very clear what the report is to include in its scope, and anything that caused debate or assumptions to be made, will need to be documented in the 'assumptions / exclusions' section of the spec so that no-one is left guessing!

 The **Key Questions** you will need answered to fill in the Scope section accurately are the '**Who**' and '**What**' that you asked in the overview Section.

4.1.2 Reference Document:

When you requested all the background information to this new requirement, you may have been sent to an original Terms of Requirement document, a Blueprint Design document, or maybe just a Change Request or an Issues Log. Any relevant reference documents such as these should be noted here. If you are working on a large project, it may be possible to insert a hyperlink to the intranet location of those documents so as not to impact the size of this spec too severely. If that is not possible, then either list the document names and the location they can be found, or embed copies of the documents (this is a last resort as those documents themselves may be updated and yours will always be as at the time you embedded it). The Implementation and Deploy Section of the template also needs to know the reference documents. Once you have documented them here in Section Four, copy and paste the same to Section 9.4 Cross Reference Documents so that the team responsible for taking the report live have all of the relevant information they need in the one section.

* * * *TOP TIP* * * *

If you have had to embed the reference documents into Section 4, then do not repeat that in the Deploy section for fear of making this spec too large to open! If this is the case, then clearly refer the Deploy section to the embedded documents in Section 4 and list the document names that they should be interested in.

*   *   *

4.1.3 Model / Process:

 The Model / Process is critical to the functional spec. As soon as you have the answers to the **Key Questions** of 'Who', 'What', 'When' and 'Where', you should be able to sketch out the relevant process flow in which the report will be run.

To do this, you need to think about what steps must be run before the report, and any steps or actions that are taken after the report is run. For instance, if the report is run nightly after all deliveries that could be dispatched have been dispatched, then the steps before executing the report will be those delivery processing steps. If the main purpose of the report is to ensure specific data has been captured prior to a subsequent processing step such as billing, then the process flow should contain the subsequent steps also to provide a complete picture.

The Process Flow should show how the report fits in to the bigger picture of what it is reporting. It does not need to be hugely detailed—basic labelled boxes and arrows will be sufficient. I usually use Microsoft PowerPoint because I find it easy and simple to use, it doesn't require a separate user license to access it (unlike more advanced tools like Visio) and most people on the project will have access to it if any changes need to be made in future. Any other process flow tool such as Visio would also be fine but my point is that you should not be spending half of your spec writing time making process flow diagrams for your document! See Part Three of this book for a good example of a Report process flow.

4.2 Controls

4.2.1 Report Description

The Report Description needs to describe in detail the answers to these questions:

- What is the purpose of the report?

- How often will it be run?

- Who will run it?

- How it will be executed?

- What output methods will be available such as printing, emailing, downloading and so on.

This is the section where you write in short, understandable sentences, the functionality that you will detail piece by piece in the Functional Solution section of the spec.

Going through this section of the spec, the reader should be able to understand what the report will contain, how it will be executed (i.e. selection screen, background job variants etc) and the intended methods of output.

Details should include the starting point for the report (i.e. after a certain business process step? Automated after the days processing is complete?), what options are available in the selection screen including mentioning mandatory fields, the type of data that the report will extract, and whether there are any custom tables that the report extraction will rely on.

4.2.2 Report Controls

In the Report Controls section, consider any legal and fiscal control requirements that may be relevant for this report. Some projects have a Control Register that might need to be updated with details of the report in those cases. Your Business Process Owner should be able to advise whether there are any applicable for this report.

 Key Questions:

- Will it display any sensitive corporate data that only specific users should have access to such as pricing structures?

- Is it country specific data that users of the same role in other countries should not see?

- Are there any other legal or fiscal control requirements relevant for this report?

- Is the report data classified as restricted (if so, in what way), or confidential?

4.2.3 Dependencies

This part of the spec is used to highlight any interdependencies with any other developments, either in progress, planned or already in existence. For instance, the report may rely on an enhancement to populate a new custom table. The enhancement needs to be referenced here so that the technical team are aware of the interdependent relationship and can plan the development of the linked objects accordingly.

If the report is dependant on an enhancement that has already been built or perhaps an inbound interface that has already advanced to Acceptance testing, it is important to list them here as dependencies in case incorrect assumptions have been made, or changes are made to those other objects that you are not aware of.

Often, country specific requirements will be dependant on each other. A good example of this is Brazil where nota fiscal information must be captured at various points in the business processes, often requiring developments to standard SAP that would need to be in existence before a new report or form could output the details accurately.

4.2.4 Access Restrictions (Security)

The Access Restrictions section should detail any authorizations or security controls that will need to be implemented with the new report. To provide the Security Team with all of the necessary information they will need to do this, you should document which business roles will need access to run the report, review or action any error logs (which may be separate transactions), or update any custom tables that the report relies on. Think about whether this will require changes to existing user roles, or the development of new roles and discuss with your Business Process Owner and Design Architect if you are not sure.

Provide the technical name of any new transactions that you want developed. Make sure you follow the naming convention provided by your project management.

* * *TOP TIP* * *

If you are not aware of a naming convention, check for other custom defined transaction codes in your development system and try and follow a similar convention for yours. In SAP, you can use transaction SE93 Display Dialog Transaction to list all transaction codes defined. The custom ones for your project may begin with 'Y', 'Z' or '/'. The technical team will always adjust the technical name you have supplied if it is not in line with their expectations.

* * *

When there are new transaction codes, make sure to outline the type of the transaction (e.g. Display, Update, Table maintenance, upload, download). If it is a table maintenance transaction, also detail the table name here.

The Security Team will need to know if the report data (and therefore execution of the report) should be restricted to just specific organizational objects such as sales organization, plant or company code. If so, then you should detail here the actual authorization object that needs to be checked, along with any specific values applicable.

For example, *The proposed authorization object is on sales organization, V_VBAK_VKO. Only users allowed to display sales organization X103 should be able to execute this report.*

*   *   * TOP TIP *   *   *

If you are not sure on what the technical name for the authorization object is, (e.g. V_VBAK_VKO) then it is fine just to describe it (e.g. Sales organization). If you want to know what the authorization object is for an existing transaction, then use transaction SE93 Display Dialog Transaction to display the details. See Figure 5A for the details of standard transaction code F110.

*   *   *

FIG. 5A Example Trxn SE93 for F110

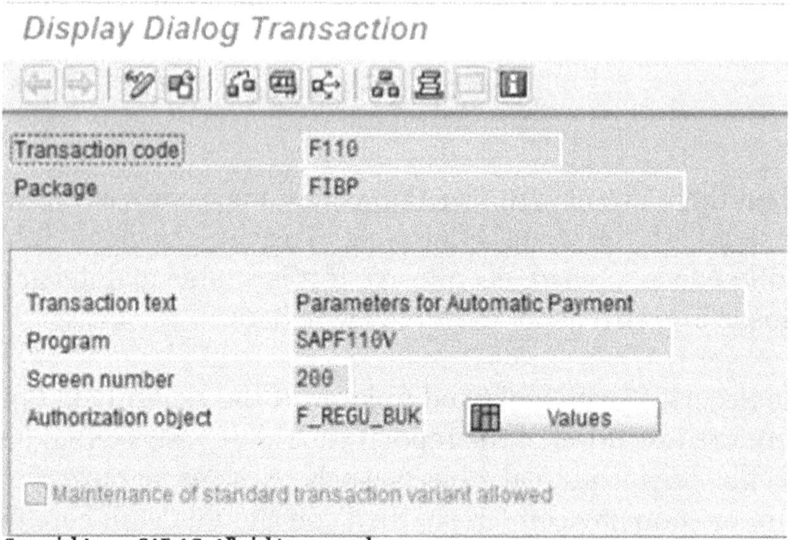

4.3 Processing

4.3.1 Starting Conditions

Quite often, your report's starting condition will simply be the preceding step in the business process. For instance, all deliveries have been despatched and post goods issued for the day so the report can be run to identify any that did not have the pre-printed number captured in XY field.

There may be reports that require specific data to have been maintained in a custom table before execution, or that will be dependant on another program having run successfully prior to this one being executed. You may also have other reports that have no specific starting condition at all—the user runs the report on an ad hoc basis. If there are definite conditions that must be met before your report is run, then list them here and include them into the Procedures for Processing in Section 9 Implementation & Deploy also. If no conditions need to be met before running the report then a statement to that effect is needed here.

 Key Questions:

- Is there any pre-requisite step that must be successfully completed before the report is run?

- Are there mandatory data requirements that must be in place first?

- Should processing of certain transactions be completed first?

- Should this report be run prior to subsequent processing taking place?

4.3.2 Frequency

Using the answer to 'When?' from your business process owner or the information gathered for the original requirement, you should be able to state how often the report will be run. If it is possible or likely that the report will be run by multiple users in the same time period, you should state that here.

This information is important to a number of teams:

The **Technical Team** will use frequency and the volume information in the next section to determine if there are likely to be performance issues, and may change their technical design accordingly.

The **Training Team** will determine the best mix of training methods (i.e. create training exercises, quick reference guides, computer based lessons etc) based on how often the report is to be run. If it is only to be run once a month, they may decide that less hands-on training exercises are required but a more detailed Support Guide will be needed instead.

The **Deploy Team** also need to know the frequency the report will be run. Will it be run on Day 1 of Go Live and therefore need onsite support? Or will it only be run at month end and require special support arrangements to cover that period? Once you have detailed the answer to when the report will be run here, copy and paste it into Section 9.1.2 Frequency in the Implementation & Deploy section so that they have all the relevant information they need to do a successful implementation of your report.

4.3.3 Volume of Data

The volume that the report program is going to have to deal with is very important but often ignored or overlooked until too late in the Project Life Cycle, usually when the testing cycle reaches an environment that has more realistic levels of transactional data in it than your development environment! Discovering performance issues that late down the track to going live is risky and expensive, often requiring a re-write of the design and re-testing under enormous time pressures.

In the Key Questions that you ask of your Business Process Owner, 'What?' should include understanding the volumes that are involved and the frequency that the report will be run. For example, daily; hourly; monthly.

What is the report showing? For instance, a report that shows deliveries that have not had a pre-printed number scanned may have to trawl through the Delivery header table, (LIKP), the item table (LIPS), and perhaps even related document tables such as SD Shipments (VTTK) or TD shipments (OIGS). If that is the case, and the report is run daily, how many deliveries and shipments of these types do the business process in a day? If the report is run monthly, how many transactional documents are added to these tables each month?

If the volume of historical data in the tables is high, then the Technical Team may highlight the report to specialised teams who monitor performance of the system. These specialists will test the report with large loads of volume to trace where the impacts are, and work with the technical team to get the most efficient technical design.

4.3.4 Archiving

Your Project may not have an archiving strategy in place when you are writing your functional spec but there are still aspects that you need to consider.

For instance, does the execution or output of the report include populating a new custom table or retrieving data from one? If the volume of data and frequency of running the report are high, then this custom table may become a performance issue over time. How much data is required to be held in these custom tables and should the Technical Team be asked to build in a removal of 'old' entries?

If only standard SAP tables are involved but historical data will add up quickly over time, then note here the main tables that the report is reliant on. Make a comment to suggest archiving of data in those tables at a future point if performance starts to suffer. This is a good professional way of recognising and documenting the future requirement, as the team supporting the report in the live environment will always come back to the functional spec for clues when there are performance issues.

Not too long ago, I was working on a global project with phased roll-outs to many countries staggered over quite a few years. Although the main SAP system was now live for the company in over ten countries, the next country to Go Live decided they needed a new report that hadn't been raised as a requirement by any of the previous countries. The report was specified and built, passed unit testing in the Development environment and was pushed through the client landscape so that the Users in this particular country could test it themselves and agree to it going live with them, the following month.

The Users failed the report miserably—they struggled to get the report results to even appear on screen as it 'timed out' almost every time it was run, regardless of how specific the selection criteria used. I was asked to step in and work with one of the technical team developers to see what the problem was, and then re-design and re-test the report so that the Users could test it and sign it off . . . . all in the space of 3 working days as we were reaching a critical 'Go / No Go' Decision for the country in question.

In my initial analysis, I found that the original functional spec hadn't considered volume of data at all. This section in the spec had been totally ignored, even though the design required the report program to wade through Shipment header tables to filter out the few shipments that met the specific criteria of the report. In our case, those shipment tables were having over 100,000 shipments added per day!

The report had tested fine in the Development environment which only had a few hundred historical shipments, but as soon as it reached a testing environment with more realistic volumes, it completely died!

Our re-design ended up using a couple of User Exits during shipment processing to populate a new custom table with relevant data when it met the specific criteria of the report. Now, when the report was run, it would extract its main data from that custom table, and then be able to make specific 'selects' on other tables to get the additional information that it needed. A lot faster to run and the Users happily signed it off, just in time!

*   *   *

4.3.5 Error Handling and Recovery Start

Think about how the report will be run, and what you want to happen should problems occur.

When the report is run in foreground by a user, you should state that meaningful error messages in the language of the user should be displayed at the Selection Screen and the Results output if applicable. You can go into detail of what the error conditions are and the actual messages you want displayed in the Functional Solution section of the spec, not here.

When the report is executed in background and fails, what do you want to happen? Should the report have an error log? Should a key business user be advised of the failure? If so, how?

These are all key questions to ask the Business Process Owner, once you have an understanding of what the report is and how it will be run.

Once you have completed this section and documented the actual error conditions and error messages in your Functional Solution, copy and paste these into section 9.1.4 Error Handling for the Deploy Team so that they do not have to wade through your whole design document to understand what errors can happen and how to address them.

4.4 Assumptions / Exclusions

I am a firm believer in 'transparency of design'! What that means is that if during the writing of my functional spec, I have some questions that maybe were not fully answered or that caused some debate amongst the business owner and design architect, whatever conclusions were drawn, agreements reached or assumptions made get documented here in this section. Then it is clear and obvious to everyone who receives a copy of the functional spec on what grounds the design has been based.

More often than not, it is usually 'exclusions' that get documented. If it is clearly documented what the report is NOT going to include, and the key people received a copy of the functional spec to review and didn't question it, then they have no recourse later down the track when the report is up and running and they decide it should have included XYZ after all! You can happily refer your Team Lead to this section and confirm that the report functional spec was signed off excluding XYZ. Those key people will now have to go through the pain and effort of raising a Change Request and justifying it, rather than trying to say it was a 'defect'!

List any assumptions that you have based your design on, and any exclusions that the report will not include in short, clear, concise bullet points.

For example:

- The report will not include Return or Inbound deliveries

- Any deliveries 30 days or older that have not yet been post goods issued will be considered 'rejected'

This section doesn't mean that you can list any unanswered questions! You need to keep asking the questions until you either get clearly defined answers that you understand and can use in your design, or where you can draw logical conclusions (assumptions) and base your design on those in which case your assumptions have to be spelt out here in case you got it wrong.

Chapter Twelve

5. Report Functional Solution

5.1 Distribution

This is the method of distribution for the report output. For instance, will it just be printed or can it also be downloaded to Microsoft Excel, emailed, auto-faxed and so on.

When the report output is to be printed, you should note here whether the output is single or double sided printing, landscape or portrait, and the type of printer (e.g. laser or dot matrix).

Are special characters required such as Cyrillic script, in which case will the output device in SAP need additional configuration? If so, you should make a note of that in the Deploy section as well since it is that team that will need to check that the users in the live environments have the correct equipment in place.

When the report output is to be emailed, do you want the user to review the results on screen first or for the output to be dispatched to the entered email address directly on execution of the report? Does the email address need to be validated prior to sending the report or will an invalid email address result in an error log of the report?

The answers to these questions may require additional selection options and functionality to be built in by the technical team.

5.2 Transaction Code

This is the transaction code proposed for the new report and should be the same as what you documented in Section 4.2.4 Access Restrictions (Security).

5.3 Selection Screen

When the report is run in foreground, the selection screen is the user's first exposure to it and it is critical to make the options available clear, understandable and detailed enough to be flexible.

Even if your report is going to be executed in background at all times, the Selection Screen is still important. It must contain enough fields for the various business areas to retrieve just the report results they are after. Often that means setting up report variants for each different business area that include their specific selection criteria.

*   *   *TOP TIP*   *   *

Another area where a consultant can make their functional spec stand out as the work of a true professional is by including a document for the 'Help / Info' icon. On standard SAP reports, the user can click on the information icon and a window will appear detailing how the report should be run. Why not do the same with yours?

*   *   *

In all of my recent projects, we have made this a standard feature for any report functional specs—the author of the spec knows why the report has been requested, how it should be executed, if there are any pre-requisites before executing the report and who (which business role) has access to run it. So once you have documented the functional solution in your spec template, copy and paste from the relevant parts into a new one page word document. I use the headings of Background, Report Description (including the different options for the report output such as printing, downloading and so on), and Access Required (mention which user roles will be assigned the report transaction code). Briefly cover what the report is, why it is needed and by whom, how to run it (point out the mandatory fields), and what the results of the report are going to show. Insert this one-pager into this section of your functional spec with a note to the technical team requesting that they copy and paste the information to sit behind the information icon on your new report's selection screen.

This section of the functional spec has three sub-sections:

- Criteria—where you will describe what selection fields will be made available

- Attributes—where you will detail how those selection fields will be used

- Elements List—where you will provide a table showing each field and its technical detail

Let's go through each in more detail now.

5.3.1 Criteria

Think through the different business areas that will use this report and how to distinguish between them. For instance, is there more than one sales area and company code that this report is relevant for? If so, then it makes sense to offer those as selection fields.

For example, company code, sales organisation, distribution channel, division.

Within each business area, will users want to report on specific products or customers, or perhaps filter the results by geographical area? Again, relate those to the relevant SAP fields and include them as selection criteria.

In addition to deciding what fields to include as criteria, think about whether they can be grouped logically on the screen to make it more understandable for the users.

For instance, you may have various fields that relate to organisational structure, (such as company code, sales organisation, plant etc) others that relate to transactional data, (such as post goods issue date, billing date, material type etc) and others that determine how the output will be generated (such as options to show the results to screen, to email, to download etc). You can arrange your selection screen with sub-headings so that the user can see at a glance the options available to them.

In this section, describe in short clear sentences:

- What fields you want to be included,

- How you want them to be grouped on the screen,

- Whether there are default values,

- Which fields will be mandatory,

- Whether multiple entries can be made to the field using ranges, inclusions, exclusions,

- Which require radial buttons for selection as opposed to input fields.

And any other aspects that you can think of that the technical team need to be aware of!

5.3.2 Attributes

I use this section of the functional spec to provide a mock-up of the layout and to add further detail with regards to what I want in the selection screen, such as the screen title, default language and so on:

- Short Description: Report for Pre-printed Number Maintenance

- Original Language: EN (English)

- Screen Type: Selection screen

- Settings: Hold scroll position

The screen layout mock-up does not have to be a work of art and it does not have to be done using SAP's Screen Painter! I usually use Microsoft PowerPoint—I put in some boxes and a bit of text, insert my chosen icons and in 20 minutes I am finished! Compare the next two figures. Figure 6A was made using transaction SE51 Screen Painter (which by the way, most of the consultants I know will not have developer key authorisations to use properly anyway!). Figure 6B was made using PowerPoint. There is not that much difference between the two but in this particular case, it took nearly an hour longer for the consultant to use Screen Painter. That's one hour less to finish off a more critical part of the functional spec!

FIG 6A SE51 SCREEN PAINTER

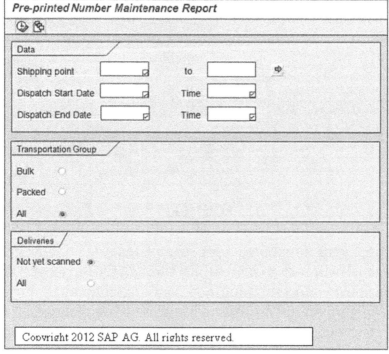

FIG 6B Screen mock-up using PowerPoint

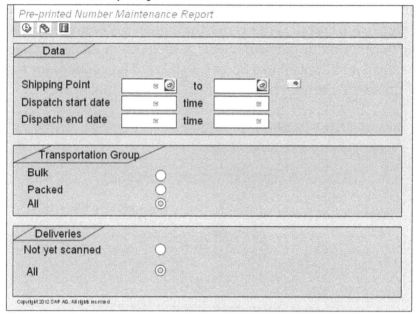

*   *   *TOP TIP *   *   *

Getting your functional spec completed to a really good standard in time to go successfully through the Review Process is the most important thing. So save yourself hours by quickly mocking up screen layouts and process flows in simple tools like Microsoft PowerPoint. Better yet, sketch them out on paper and get someone else to fiddle with the boxes in PowerPoint for you while you continue on other sections!

*   *   *

Amongst your consultant's 'toolkit' of useful SAP bits and pieces that you take with you from project to project, I suggest that if you don't already have them, make up a one page word document with all the useful SAP icons as jpeg images. That way, you can quickly and easily copy and paste the relevant icons from the word document into your PowerPoint mock-ups. You will find some ready made lists on the internet such as these:

http://www.sapdesignguild.org/resources/icons_sap/index. htm

http://myhelp.uky.edu/rwd/HTML/QRC/QRC_Icons_Advanced_v2.pdf

5.3.3 Elements List

In this section, you now need to go through the selection screen field by field and clearly state the field name, type, length and so on. I suggest using a table format that includes the following:

Field description:

The text you want to show next to a field. Be conscious of the maximum length available for text descriptions. If necessary, abbreviate but make sure that the result is still clearly understandable to the Users. For example, Ship Pt rather than Sh Point.

Field:

The technical field name from the appropriate SAP table. For example, VSTEL

Check Table:

Should the value entered in the field be validated against entries in another table? For example, shipping point selection field should be validated against the configured list of shipping points in table TVST

Field Type:

Classify each field on the selection screen appropriately as a label, for input, a radial button, and so on.

Format:

For each selection field, state the format of the value entered. Your usual choices will be CHAR, DATS or TIMS.

Length:

Put the length of the SAP field. For instance, shipping point is CHAR format of length 4. Any selection fields being pulled from a custom table may have non-standard lengths so be sure to check against the table details using transaction SE11 so that the technical team allow enough screen space for each field.

Mandatory Field:

A yes or no will do. Where the user is able to enter a range of values and it is also a mandatory field, make sure that you include testing with single values, ranges, and non-consecutive values in your unit testing.

Default Values:

Should any of the fields be pre-populated with a default value? If so, you need to provide the Technical Team with details on how to determine that default.

Comments:

Sometimes additional explanation may be needed for some of the fields with regards to the logic for default value determination or perhaps the format required. I suggest that you use Notes. That is, in the comment field of your Elements List table, say 'See Note 1' and then below the table, detail the additional information for Note 1. In this way, you are not trying to cram too much detail into the elements list table and it is very clear to the Technical Team where to look for the extra information.

Make sure you cover every single field you are requesting on your Selection screen. Think through whether the user can enter multiple selections for each field, the formatting of the field (i.e. will date fields be DDMMYY or DDMMYYYY or YYYYMM etc), any default entries required, any validations needed, and any logic that might be required to calculate the content of a field.

5.4 Data Extraction Criteria

This is the really important meaty part of the functional spec. You have already covered the Why, When and Who of the new report. Now you are going to detail exactly what you want the technical team to produce for you. You have just given them all the details they need to create the Selection Screen. So the next step is to start documenting what happens when the user has completed the selection screen and hits 'execute'.

Think the new report through logically. You know from your detailed design analysis what fields the report should show and in what order they should appear in the results. From which table should the technical team start the extraction? What logic should they use? How will the selection screen criteria impact the logic? From the initial table, which tables are next and how should they filter down the data to match the user requirement?

These are not easy questions to answer and it is critical that you make this section as clear and easy to follow as possible to avoid mistakes. Start with a simple diagram showing the extraction criteria so that at a glance, the reader of the spec can see which table the logic should begin with, and then the other tables that are extracted from and the decisions made. (See Part 3 Fig 10C for a good example of an extraction logic diagram.) Also document any new custom tables that might be required as part of the design. Then move on to the sub-sections in this part of the functional spec to capture all the finer details.

5.4.1 Fields in the Report

Create a table in your spec with columns for Field Description, Column heading, Field, Type, Length, Position and Comments.

Field Description:

In this table column, list out every field required in your report results.

Column Heading:

Put in the description that you want to appear in the column heading. Remember to provide clear abbreviations and be mindful of the column length of the actual data. For instance, you don't want to ask for a 30 char column heading where the contents will only be 4 characters long unless you know your report will have plenty of space in the layout available to accommodate it.

Consider also whether your report will be run in more than one language. If so, you will need to provide the Technical

Team with the column headings to be used for each applicable language and advise how they are to determine the language to be used. That is, should they use the language specified on the selection screen or the default language of the report user?

Field:

Detail the table and field name in SAP

Type:

This is the field type. Your usual choices will be CHAR, DATS or TIMS.

Length:

Put the length of the SAP field. For instance, shipping point is CHAR format of length 4, so this table cell would hold '4'. Any selection fields being pulled from a custom table may have non-standard lengths so be sure to check against the table details using transaction SE11 so that the technical team allow enough screen space for each field.

Position:

Use your own numbering system to relate this report field with the layout mock-up that you are going to provide later in the functional spec. If your report is going to be ALV format, then this might simply be the column number. However if your report is a unique format, it will help the Technical Team accurately determine where the information is to be shown if you provide a number here and then show that number in the correct position on your layout mock-up.

Comments:

If the extraction logic is simple for the field, then detail it here within the table. For example, report column 'Contract', Field VBAK-BSTKD, the comments might be 'retrieve the contract purchase order number from this field.'

If the extraction is a text, consider any alternative languages that the user may run the report in. Should the field content in the report be retrieved in that language also?

If the extraction logic is more complex, then refer to Note 1 and then beneath your table, document in more detail the logic required for Note 1. Provide a Note reference for every field that requires more than just a simple field extraction.

See below for an example:

Note 1. Extraction criteria for retrieving Delivery Number

Using the Shipping Point, Dispatch Start/End Date and Time and Transportation Group, get all the deliveries for the dates entered in the selection criteria.

If Transportation Group TRAGR = 0001 (Packed Lubes Deliveries)

> *Find Actual GI Date LIKP-WADAT_GI and Actual GI Time LIKP-OIWATIM and display those deliveries that match the selection criteria entered by the user.*

> *Check if LIKP-OIHNOTWERKS is populated, if populated this indicates the delivery is an intercompany delivery else it's a normal delivery.*

* * * TOP TIP * * *

A functional consultant should not write code, build tables, design efficient database retrievals, or decide that one BAPI, function module, class, or IDOC is better than another.

It is not appropriate and quite risky for you to decide these technical details or to put pseudo code in your functional spec. It is your responsibility to describe clearly where the technical team should find the data, and how that data should be filtered and formatted for the report. It is the Technical Team's responsibility to determine the best code and technical design needed to get those results. If you cross the line by putting pseudo code in your spec, you will risk that code being implemented without consideration for whether it is the best fit, good for performance, or even accurate!

* * *

5.4.2 Error Handling

In this section, you need to document in detail the error handling procedure that you want the technical team to implement. This may differ between report formats.

Insert a simple table here that lists the Error condition on the left and the error message that you want on the right of it. For example, if the shipping point is a mandatory selection field and has not been filled in, your error condition might be 'shipping point not entered' and your error message 'Enter shipping point'.

If the report can be run in multiple languages, then not only does the selection screen, output fields and column names need to be translated, but also your error messages. If this is the case, it often helps to use standard text (transaction SO10) to capture the translations in the various languages and then detail in your spec how to retrieve the correct one.

5.4.3 Report Output Format

Consider every possible output that the report can be produced in. For each of these, describe the format, any special logic to be used, and provide a mock-up example.

For instance, if the report is to be run to screen in ALV format with a header detailing the date and time of running and the user details, how will that look when downloaded to Microsoft Excel?

If the report can be emailed directly to either an SAP Inbox or an external email address, what format should the report take and what subject line should be used? Should there be a message in the email body or will the attachment and subject line be sufficient?

For each format, consider and document:

- The layout to be used including font, size, colour

- Whether the data can be refreshed within the report

- Report header information

- Report item details

- Page numbering

- Orientation

- File types

- Printer types

- What to show if a column is completely blank

- Whether columns can be moved

5.4.4 Sorting Sequence

Document the sorting sequence required. If data in the results can have multiple records shown in the report, you may need to specify sorting sequences across the columns.

Chapter Thirteen

6. Testing Requirements

I can't stress enough how important Unit Testing is to any new or changed development. This is the very first stage of testing—it is by far the most economical and best time to flush out any bugs in the development and ensure that all features and benefits of the design are accurately included.

- Documenting Test Cases prevents oversight

- Documentation clearly indicates the quality of test cases

- When the development needs to be retested, we can be sure nothing is missed

- It provides a level of transparency of what was really tested during unit testing.

- It helps in knowledge transfer in case of consultant attrition

- Unit Test Cases can be used to develop test cases for other levels of testing

So, who is responsible for what in this stage of testing?

The Consultant's Unit Test responsibility:

- Document the Test Requirements

- Create Test Plans, with Test Cases and Test Data

- Identify the 'bigger picture' business processes the report will need testing in

- Once the developer has handed over the development, execute the test cases

- Document and re-assign any bugs or discrepancies

- Repeat the test cycle until the report or "unit" is free of all bugs

*   *   * *TOP TIP* *   *   *

Remember, as the consultant responsible for the Functional Spec, you may not be the actual unit tester executing the test cases. You must ensure that all the requirements are adequately covered in at least one test case, and that the steps to execute and capture actual results are very clear. Regardless of whether the developer has 'unit tested' the report before handing it over, or how well you know and trust him or her, unit testing the report is the ultimate responsibility of functional consultants / analysts within the SAP project life cycle, and must be executed, documented, and proven successful before it can be 'signed off' for moving through the development life cycle and the other Test environments.

*   *   *

The Technical Team Unit Test responsibility:

- Make sure that all of the Test Requirements are covered accurately in the development build

- Understand the basics of the business process that needs this development so that the focus is accurate and relevant test data is used during development.

- Test that the key requirements are met before handing over the development for formal unit testing.

- Address and fix bugs in a timely, effective manner, ensuring they won't 're-appear' later in the development life cycle.

What makes up a unit test?

- One or more Test Plans

- With one or more Test Cases

- Including multiple Test Requirements and the relevant Test Data to execute them

What is a Test Plan?

Your test plan will document a number of test cases that together, prove that the functional requirements in your specification have been successfully met. It will describe how the tests will be carried out, in which environment, any prerequisites, assumptions, other impacted developments, roles and high level steps.

For the Report Functional Specification, we should have a test plan for each of the sub sections of requirements that we have identified.

For instance, a test plan for the 'selection screen' will document all the test cases relevant to making sure that the selection screen layout is correct, that all the fields work as expected, and that all the features we have listed as 'test requirements' are accurately included. There should be other test plans for the 'report execution and layout' and each of the other report sub sections that are relevant. These should ensure that all of the features and functionality we have requested are fully tested.

What is a Test Case?

A test case is a mini scenario or set of transactions that are run with specific data to meet the test requirements that it needs to test. It's a set of test conditions (i.e. the specific data being used) that will determine if the aspect of the report you are testing is working as per your design in your functional specification.

Simply put, a test case describes exactly how the test should be carried out.

For example the test case may describe a test as follows:

Step 1: Type 10 characters in the Name Field

Step 2: Click on Execute

In order to prove that your report meets all of the requirements in your functional specification, you will need to include both positive and negative test cases.

For example, a positive test such as 'the report executes to screen successfully with these valid selection criteria', and a negative test 'the report returns an error message when invalid selection criteria are used'.

Your test cases should start with inputs such as which selection criteria to fill in and with what values. Note, you can pre-save selection variants for each test case and then refer to the variant name so that the unit tester does not have to key the values each time.

It should also include steps for processing, such as whether the tester should execute the report to screen, or whether an alternative output method such as direct to printer or email is to be used.

Finally, your test cases must include the results that you expect the tester to have, such as:

- Selection criteria entered successfully without errors;

- Execution of the report returned the output to the screen within xx number of seconds;

- Report output included all relevant data for the selection criteria entered;

- No invalid records were returned

See Appendix A for more details on the format of your test plans and test cases.

What is a Test Requirement?

A requirement is a statement that identifies a necessary attribute, function, or characteristic, for it to have value and use to the end user. For your report functional spec, you should group your test requirements into sub sections for each major element of your report.

I've listed the common areas (sub sections) here:

- 6.1 Selection Screen

- 6.2 Report Execution and Layout

- 6.3 Report Content

- 6.4 Custom Tables

- 6.5 Authorisations

- 6.6 Test Data

- 6.7 Other Test Cycles

These are the key elements of your new report and are included as such in the Report Functional Spec template. You may need to copy, paste and rename to add extras or you may decide that one of these is not relevant for your report. In that case, you can either put N/A for not applicable, or you can delete that sub section from your spec template. For example, if your report development has not needed any new custom tables to be defined then you would not need that sub section in your spec.

For each of these testing requirement areas, you need to list the key aspects and functionality that **must be unit tested**.

These are the features and requirements of your report. I usually bullet point these per section so that I can build my test cases around them. I aim to have a unit test plan with many test cases for each testing requirement area.

In this section of your functional spec, bullet point the key aspects of your report under each of these sub sections that must be unit tested successfully.

In Appendix A, you will need to create a Test Plan for each sub section, and then within each test plan, build the bullet points of key aspects from this section, into actual test cases to prove that the functionality works as per your design.

Let's work through these sub sections and then see how it fits together into your test plans and test cases for Appendix A.

6.1 Selection Screen

Everything about the selection screen must be unit tested. List the key aspects here as follows so that you can incorporate them easily into your test plan later.

For Example:

- Layout of selection screen is as per detailed design in section 5 of this spec

- Radial buttons can be activated

- Multiple values can be entered for every field

- Default values are correct

- Invalid field entries are not accepted

- Mandatory fields cannot be left empty

- Optional fields can be left empty

- Selection screen variants can be created, retrieved and changed

.... and so on. This is going to be a very big list but it is really important to brainstorm as much as possible into it so that you remember to include test cases that cover off every single aspect, and so that the Technical Team are fully aware of what you are expecting their development to provide.

* * * TOP TIP * * ⁎*

Don't forget to test: mandatory versus optional fields, negative tests, all possible types of values for each field such as alpha, numeric, sequential and non-sequential ranges, exclusions and so on. Include test cases to verify the spelling, font and size of all the "labels" or text that appears on the screen. Error messages should also be tested along with any other functionality you have requested such as the ability to create, change, retrieve and delete selection screen variants.

* * *

6.2 Report Execution and Layout

Report execution testing means testing every different way or method that the report can be run. Work back through the Detailed Design in section 5 of your specification. Make a list of all the different methods of execution that you have requested from the technical team. For instance, you may have included executing the report in the foreground to the user's screen, executing in background, executing and sending via email, printing single sided to a Laser Printer and so on.

For each of these different execution methods, you need to list here the testing requirements. For example:

- Report can be executed to screen

- Report can be printed to a specified Laser printer

- Report can be downloaded to an Excel file

- Report can be sent by email

- Only valid external email addresses can be used

- Email subject line is as per detailed design requirements

- Attachment in the email is 'read only'

- Attachment in the email can be opened without error

- Attachment in the email is in the correct layout

And so on. Your report will need many more requirements than just these! These are the 'requirements' that you need to make sure the developer has accurately understood and provided in the new report.

Here are some more key points to think about and include in your design, and in your list of test requirements where applicable:

Printing—have you specified the type of printing of the report? Will it be standard single side printing? Will it be double sided printing? Will it be dot matrix flow printing? Should the report be printed on headed paper? Will a default printer be used and if so, where is this maintained? Can the user overwrite a default printer?

Emailing the Report—What does your specification say about email addresses that can be used? Will there be a validity check on any email address entered that needs to be tested? Will the report program need to retrieve an email address from master data? Will the report be sent to only SAP internal email addresses, to only external email addresses, or to any valid email address? Make sure you include negative as well as positive test requirements to be sure the functionality is working as per your specification.

With regards to layout, you will need to ensure that the layout in every method of execution is fully tested. Go through each method of execution one by one and add test requirements to your list for the layout requirements for each method. Be thorough—for each execution method, you will need to make sure that the layout is as per the original user requirements that you have documented in your detailed design.

For downloads to Excel, include requirements that the file produced can be opened without errors, saved to the user's preferred location, are read-only if applicable.

For emailed reports, ensure that layout requirements include testing that the structure of the email, including the subject line and body, are as per your design.

Test the structure of the report—is your report hierarchical (drill down) or control break (divided into sections and/ or sub-sections)? Ensure these aspects are covered in test cases and that special attention is paid to headings, sub-headings, and footers included in each layout as per your functional specification.

Layout unit testing should also include checking that every column of data expected is shown, and that when no valid data for a column is extracted, that the displayed result is as you expect (i.e. blank or with a zero or whatever).

6.3 Report Content

Make sure that every piece of data extracted and output for the selection criteria entered, matches your test expectations. The test plan, test cases and test data used are crucial to decent unit testing. In this section, I would bullet point the key points.

For example:

- All data extracted and output for the selection criteria entered meets the extraction rules defined in section 5 of this spec

- When no valid data is extracted for a column, the field content is blank (or whatever you have specified)

- When no data is extracted at all, an error message to that effect is displayed

- All calculated fields are accurate

- Rounding of totals are as per the design specified (Be very careful if sub-totals are added together to calculate a Grand Total, that that value is 'true' and rounding has not caused a discrepancy.)

And so on, remembering to include tests on all possible error messages and execution methods to ensure that the report content is accurate and consistent across all of them. The emphasis for the test cases covering report content will be on ensuring that the data (selection criteria) the tester uses, has known, exact expected results for each and every field and column in the report. The effort is in preparing the test data and test cases properly so that test execution is a simple task of checking the actual results match the expected results and capturing proof!

6.4 Custom Tables

In Section Five Detailed Design, you may have requested that a new custom table be defined to hold data needed for this report. If not, then mark this section in your functional spec as 'not applicable' and move on to section 6.5 Authorisations.

However, if you have requested a new custom table to be defined to support this report, then you must ensure you include a test plan with test cases specific to testing not only the table contents, but also the table structure and maintenance.

For example, test requirements for a custom table supporting a report may include:

- New entries can be created in the table

- Table Entries can be changed

- Table entries can be deleted

- Table entries can be displayed

- Only valid table entries can be saved

- All entries must be unique

- Table entries are accurately retrieved and reported

6.5 Authorisations

The security team may not provide a test user id in time for your unit test of the development. Detailing the testing requirement in your spec means that it can be properly tested when it is made available. Read through the following concepts for authorisation testing and then list your testing requirements to ensure that you have covered all of these bases.

Security or authorisation testing is a process to determine that an information system protects data and maintains functionality as intended. That is, that our new SAP report protects data and functions as our design intended.

The six basic security concepts that need to be covered by security testing are:

Confidentiality

A security measure which protects against the disclosure of information to parties other than the intended recipient. So, include a requirement in your testing that makes sure that only those business roles that should have access to the report can run it, and that other roles cannot. That is, both a positive and a negative test requirement.

Integrity

A measure intended to allow the receiver to determine that the information which it is provided with is correct. This means making sure that the validity of the report output is not impacted by the security or authorisation changes. For instance, if the Financial Controller Role is allowed to run the report for all company codes, then the report output should include all relevant data for all company codes. Adversely, if the Financial Controller is only authorised to report for a single company code, the report output should be restricted accordingly too.

Authentication

For our purposes, this would involve confirming the identity of a person through the login and password. That is, once the security team has issued you with a test user login and password, use that to login and test the report authorisations, not your own personal login and password.

Authorisation

The process of determining that a user is allowed to run the report and view, send, or disseminate the output. Again, once the security team has issued you with a test user login and password, use that to login and test the report authorisations, not your own personal login and password.

Availability

Assuring information and communications services will be ready for use when expected. Information must be kept available to authorised persons when they need it. This is common sense—if your business requirements are that the business roles need to run this report on an ad hoc basis, then they should not be restricted to only running the report at month end or after other processing has been completed.

Non-repudiation

In reference to digital security, non-repudiation means to ensure that a transferred message has been sent and received by the parties claiming to have sent and received the message. Non-repudiation is a way to guarantee that the sender of a message cannot later deny having sent the message and that the recipient cannot deny having received the message. So, if your new report is to allow sending of the output by Email, then your testing should include a check to make sure that the outbound message records who instigated it (i.e. the user running the report), when, and to whom it was sent. Also include a test to verify that the email was received only by the recipient email address.

6.6 Test Data

Specify what test data is available for the report and in which testing environment it can be found. For Reports, this is often an easier task than it is for other types of development but you will still need to think about what is necessary for a unit test by the developers, the functional consultant assigned to the unit testing and any key users in the testing environment.

Do not be lazy here! If you put a little bit of effort in here, you will save yourself a lot of time and frustration later by making sure that everyone has the data they need up front.

Your test data must be:

1. Realistic

    By realistic, it means the data should be accurate in the context of real life e.g if the report will normally be run weekly and list all deliveries supplied from a range of plants, and there are usually around 1500 of these per week, limiting your test data to a single delivery or a single plant is not a realistic test. This also means identifying more than one of each 'object' for use in testing. That is, more than one material, customer, plant, company code, sales area and so on.

2. Practically Valid

This is similar to realistic but not the same. This property is more related to the business logic. If most deliveries are made from just 5 of the possible 15 plants, then it makes sense for most of your test data to be from those 5 plants.

3. Versatile

Think about the test requirements you have covered under each of the sub sections. Select test data that covers as many of these as possible. For instance, if test data only exists for a one month period for some plants but for many sequential months for other plants, then choose the more versatile data.

4. Exceptional

In addition to choosing practical and valid data, think about any exceptions that you may need to test. For instance, if the majority of business units running the report will generate multi page outputs, but one of the business units has a very slow turnover and will only generate single page reports each time it is run, then include test data for this exception to ensure that the report is accurate for both single and multi page outputs.

A tester should not try to justify any bug saying that test data was not available or was incomplete. It's your responsibility to create or find your own test data according to the testing requirements. Be very careful when relying on the test data created by another tester as it may not be set up accurately for your testing needs.

*   *   *TOP TIP *   *   *

Use table browsing (transaction SE16N / SES16) to try and find relevant data. List the relevant valid data for each field in the selection screen. In this way, the developer can check here to find valid entries to use, and then quickly enter the data to test what he needs to without coming back to you with questions all the time. Think also about data dependencies such as whether stock is in place for a goods issue, whether standard texts have been defined and so on. Remember, you want to put the effort into your test data once so that it is then self-sufficient and can be used repeatedly without your manual intervention.

*   *   *

In some rare cases, fresh test data may need to be prepared just prior to running the report. For instance if the report outputs deliveries that have been picked but not post goods issued, and all valid test data of that status have been processed too far to be used. In this case, think carefully about whether test data can be 'rolled back' to the relevant status (i.e. reverse the goods issue of the delivery to return it to the required status), or whether it is better to identify partially processed deliveries and carry them forward to the 'picked' status.

In either scenario, if test data does not exist, then you will need to list the steps necessary to create test data required to test the report. Please provide valid data and the menu paths necessary to execute the transaction. This includes company codes, sales organizations, document types, plants, G/L accounts, etc. An example is listed below.

Transaction: VL06O List Outbound Deliveries

Step 1: Use selection criteria of supplying plants A100 to A500, delivery type ZLF, picking status A and execute

Step 2: From the results, drill in to Change Delivery and update the relevant storage location and pick quantity to bring the picking status to C. Save each delivery

Step 3: Make a note of the supplying plants that the updated deliveries have been picked from and use those plants as selection criteria in the report.

6.7 Other Test Cycles

Although Section Six of your functional specification template mainly involves preparing and documenting for Unit Testing, once successfully signed off, your report will go on to be Acceptance Tested, included in Integration Testing, perhaps Quality Assurance tested, or Performance tested. And even once it is live in Production, any future changes to it will need Regression Testing!

Don't worry, the scope of this book doesn't go that far! But what you do need to think about and include in your functional spec is an outline of the business process that this report is part of, so that the appropriate Acceptance / Integration / QA test scenario can be identified. You will have completed this as part of Section 4.1.3 Model / Process. So here, all you need to do is to have a look at your project's library of Acceptance or Integration Test scripts and see which one(s) are valid for having this report included in them. Then list the names of those test scripts in this section of your functional spec template. If you cannot find any scripts where your report would logically slip into the process described, or if your project does not yet have any Acceptance or Integration test scripts documented, then you will need to refer readers of your spec to the model / process documented in Section 4.1.3. Suggest that these next phases of testing follow those steps to ensure a thorough end to end process test for your report.

Why is this important? Remember that the functional spec will live on, long past your involvement in it. Other teams in the project will need to refer to this section of your spec to understand how the report fits in with the business processes that real users do in their real jobs. The Training team, the Deploy team, and the Support team will all find this information necessary and useful.

Chapter Fourteen

7. Issues

When you first write your functional spec, this section can be left blank. I can hear you cheer from here! This section is used mainly after the new report has gone live in Production, or at least after development has begun. That is because we use this section to keep track of any issues that are raised or changes requested, after the initial development has been signed off. Let's take a closer look at what these might be:

Technical Issues:

During development, the technical consultant may find a problem with meeting the requirements in the way that the design has been specified. This is particularly common where the functional consultant has over-stepped the boundary and stated technical design details in their functional design document! Remember, if the functional design and business requirements are clearly documented, then the functional consultant does not need to step into 'technical' descriptions and can leave the technical design solely to the experts who should be trusted to choose the best possible technical solution to meet them, resolving potential issues of them trying to do it 'your way'.

Sometimes the technical issues only appear when the development has been moved to a larger, more densely populated environment for testing. That is often when the technical design is found to have performance problems because perhaps the more realistic volume of data was not considered as part of the functional design.

Business Issues:

Very occasionally, the business sponsor or owner, or their testing representatives may raise a business issue with the new report during one of the testing cycles. This could be caused by a number of reasons. Perhaps the original business owner has changed and the current owner has different expectations, or it may just be that since this is the first time the business are getting to see their report and use it, that they realise they have missed some requirements out or that our functional consultant has mis-interpreted some requirements. These types of issues usually start out as a testing defect, only to have someone check the functional spec and advise that the issue was not part of the original design. That usually leads to some discussion as to whether the issue is critical or not, and depending on your project, the budget, the project timescale and available resources, it may turn from an 'issue' into a Change Request.

Change Requests:

These can originate from technical or business issues, or from testing defects where it's been found that the current design does not adequately meet the business requirements. In any case, a Change Request is raised and when approved, should be documented in this section for future reference.

When you do need to update a functional spec with an Issues section, follow these guidelines to ensure the spec is updated clearly, and can easily be understood.

- Create a subsection for the issue

  The first issue in this section will be subsection 7.1, the second issue will be 7.2 and so on.

- Give the issue a clear and concise title

  The title of the issue should include whether it is a Technical Issue or a Change Request (remember that business issues will turn into Change Requests once approved so fall under this category), the associated issue or Change Request number and a short description of the topic.

- Give the issue a Background

  Briefly outline the background to the issue or change request that includes how the issue was found, what the issue is, and the impact.

- Document the agreed Resolution

  Summarise the main changes that are required to resolve the issue and include hyperlinks to the relevant sections of your functional spec that are being updated to reflect this change.

*   *   * TOP TIP *   *   *

Microsoft Word allows us to put in hyperlinks to jump from one part of our word document to another. This is really useful for your functional spec when you are updating various sections as a result of a change request. You can summarise the changes required here under Resolution, and then add a hyperlink to each part of the change that will take the reader directly to the relevant updated part of the spec.

To do this, firstly go to the updated section of your functional spec that you want to 'jump' to, for instance *Section 5.4.1 Fields in the Report.* Highlight the text or a heading and then go to Insert > Bookmark on your Word document menu path. Give your bookmark a name such as Section541. Don't use any spaces in the bookmark name or start with numbers as it won't like it. Click 'Add' to create the bookmark.

Now go back to Section 7 of your functional spec, to the Resolution where you describe the change to be made affecting that section. Select the text that you want to display as a hyperlink.

Go to Insert > Hyperlink on your Word document menu path. Choose 'place in this document'. Find your Bookmark and click on that and then 'okay'.

Congratulations, you have now linked your Section 7 changes directly to the updated section 5 of your functional spec! Any reader of the spec can now click on the hyperlink shown in your Resolution and be taken directly to the updated design. If you get stuck with hyperlinks, use the Microsoft Word help. Remember to put hyperlinks into your section 7 for every updated section of your functional spec.

*   *   *

Here is an example of how Section 7 could look like:

7.1 Technical Issue 173 re Performance

Background

During Acceptance Testing in environment A94, users complained that the report was taking over ten minutes to run, regardless of the selection criteria used. Subsequent investigations by the Technical team have found that the Select statements on some of the tables are hampered by the volume of data in those tables. Tech issue 173 has been raised to cover defects 112, 115 and 117.

Resolution

The following changes will be made to address the performance issue:

- Transactional date range will be a mandatory selection criterion. Refer to updated sections 4.3.3 Volume of Data, 5.3.1 Criteria, 5.3.3 Elements List

- A validation check will be included to ensure the date range entered does not exceed 31 days. Refer to updated sections 5.4.2 Error Handling and section 8 Tech spec

- Select statements on the LIKP and LIPS tables will be reviewed Refer to updated section 8 Tech spec

*   *   * TOP TIP *   *   *

The functional spec should always reflect the latest design. So that means that when a change request or an issue results in a change to the design that was originally documented, in addition to updating this section as described, the functional consultant must CHANGE the relevant sections of the functional spec so that it reflects the latest design. That means actually changing the wording of the affected parts of the functional spec as if this 'change' was part of the original design. It does not mean appending paragraphs or comments to those sections in highlighted fonts referencing the change request or issue number! The only section in the functional spec that should refer to a change request, issue or defect number is this section and the document semantics section at the very front of the spec that shows when the document was updated, by whom and why. All other changes should be seamless to the reader.

*   *   *

Chapter Fifteen

8. Technical Specification

In the early days of SAP implementations, there was only one spec. How technical it was depended on who wrote it. Any documentation the developers wrote afterwards to really plan how they were going to implement it was informal and often remained on white-boards or notepads. Yet in order to ensure the project would proceed without hazard and on time and on budget, the documentation needed to be more technical. Such detailed technical specifications took time—time wasted if the goals and function of the development should change or fail to gain approval.

This problem was tackled as more and more seasoned developers and experienced functional consultants moved into SAP implementations. They brought with them new standards for documentation that helped ensure more accurate plans and less technical problems. They introduced a division in the design document between goals and method, and between function and technique. They separated the design document into the functional specification and technical specification. This way, the clients, users or principal designers of the development could review the functional specification and approve the goals and functions of the proposed change, whether it was a new report, enhancement, form or interface—leaving the determination and documentation of the methods and technique up to the technical team of developers.

Therefore, the technical team waited until the functional specification was approved and signed-off before starting on the technical specification. They worked from the functional specification alone, ignoring any design changes that occurred after sign-off unless the spec was updated and a new schedule agreed to. The division saved time for the developers and gave them more control of the schedule, while still ensuring they had a complete plan for the methods and technique for implementation.

Although some companies still refer to the functional specification as the "design document" and produce a separate technical specification, it is becoming more standard to include the technical spec within the functional design document so that there is only one document in circulation and to be kept current.

In short, *what goes into the report* and *what it does* is documented in the functional specification sections of the template. This is often written from the perspective of the user. *How* it is implemented and *how* it performs the function is documented in the technical specification section. This is often written from the system perspective. Both form important deliverable milestones in the design stage of the development process.

So, this section should outline in more detail the technical solution for the report. This will be completed by the technical consultant after the functional spec has been signed off and should contain information such as pseudo code, detailed database selects, complex calculations and conversions, critical decision logic and so on. It should also outline performance considerations, and any additional authorisation checks that need to be included.

The technical consultant should request assistance from the functional consultant as required. This section should help to ensure that the technical consultant has understood the functional design, and can convey the development requirements to the developers. If additional technical documentation is available but not included in this document, then cross-reference to it here.

I joined a small project team a number of years ago, taking over from a functional consultant who was moving on. This project had been systematically rolling out a small SAP implementation across business units for a couple of years, and my role was to continue extending the Sales and Distribution design to the next business units, while supporting the business units that had recently gone live should they have any defects or issues that needed addressing.

It was a busy but friendly project team and everything was going fine until I was assigned a defect for a custom Report where the latest users felt their data was not being reflected correctly. I couldn't locate any functional spec on the report, nor any clear test plans or cases that had been used to unit test it. I was running 'blind' and relying heavily on my own testing and what the users were telling me as I did not have a clue what the original intentions were for the column in the report that they were not happy with!

Eventually I sat down with the project team's one ABAP developer to try and understand the history. He told me that as it was such a small project team, when he started with them two years previously, no formal documentation was being made for any developments or configuration. Basically, a functional consultant would approach him to discuss their requirements in an informal way, and then would send him an email summarising what was required. Andy would develop based on the email, hand it over for testing and most of the time, not have too many requests for re-work.

After some investigation, he found some old emails with the original 'requirements', plus some relating to past defects. With these emails and his help looking at the actual code being used, I managed to cobble together a basic functional spec that described the report's original purpose, use, and functionality. Andy summarised the technical spec in this new document and I contacted the users to talk them through it. As it turned out, the latest users had simply misunderstood the source of the report data and were more than happy to close the defect once I was able to talk them through the functional spec that now documented the original requirements! After a quick chat with the rest of the project team, we all decided to implement the basic functional spec design for new developments going forward to avoid the same problems reoccurring in future. Another happy ending!

* * *

Chapter Sixteen

9. Implementation & Deploy

Towards the beginning of my SAP career, functional specifications, if they were written at all, focussed mainly on providing enough detail (table names, field types and so on) for the ABAP developer to create something. In recent years, the professional management consultancies are taking a more integrated view of their documentation, and considering the wider audience. Remember way back in Chapter Two? Other roles in your project team will need to understand your new report to:

- Prepare training materials for the end Users,

- Action cutover activities

- Communicate to the Business about oncoming changes

- Prepare for Go Live

- Support the end Users once the report is live

Regardless of whether this report will be a major or a minor change, whether the users are all in a single business unit or spread across many, there needs to be a shared understanding among those driving the implementation of what needs to be done to ensure a successful go live. That is why I have this section in all of my functional specifications—so that I can give detailed information on the new report relevant for each site or business unit that is going to implement it.

This section of the functional spec template has four main sections—User Instructions, SAP Job Definitions, Issues, and Cross Reference documents. Within each of these sections, there are many sub-sections to provide a structured approach to providing this valuable information to the team(s) that will take your report to a successful implementation.

9.1 User Instructions

Refer to the functional spec template for each of the sub-headings. You will at least need to consider each of these for relevance before moving on to the next part of your spec writing.

In the 'procedures for processing' section, you need to provide clear steps for running the report. For instance, is the first step running the report transaction or should the user first check a custom table entry or their user profile defaults? Check back to section 4.3.1 Starting Conditions and document the steps here. The following example is sufficient detail:

Step 1 Execute transaction ZD11 to call up the report.

Step 2 Retrieve Selection Variant for business area by following menu path GoTo>Variants>Get.

Step 3 Select required output method. Put valid directory location and file name if outputting directly to Excel. Enter valid email address if outputting to email.

Step 4 Execute

Remember to mention if any user defaults, selection variants, email addresses or other master data needs to be set up prior to the report execution. This also includes any printers that may need special configuration.

This section also has a 'frequency' sub-heading, which you will have completed in section 4.3.2. The Deploy Team need to know the frequency the report will be run. Will it be run on Day 1 of Go-live and therefore need on-site support? Or will it only be run at month end and require special support arrangements to cover that period? Copy the relevant details from your section 4.3.2 to this section so that the team deploying your report are fully aware of when the report will be executed.

In the unlikely event that your SAP system is down, or that this specific report cannot be executed due to a bug not yet fixed or some other reason, you will need to consider the requirement for and feasibility of manual procedures.

Consider what you have documented in the report overview and in section 4 under the business units impacted and the report description.

- How critical is this report information to the business?

- Is it a legal requirement?

- How often is the report run and when?

If the report is of critical importance, is run on a frequency that is disrupted by the SAP system or report not being available, and there are other methods of obtaining the information required, then you will need to document here the 'workaround' or manual steps required.

For example, if the problem is with the actual report program, the manual steps to retrieve the report results may require running table browses and downloading those results to Excel, and then manually applying the filtering and selection process logic that the report code usually does for you. List the steps briefly but clearly, in a logical order. To be truly thorough, you could test the effectiveness of your manual steps by comparing the results from the execution of the report with those prepared from the manual steps. The sign of a true professional consultant is one who will put the thought and effort into quickly documenting how to handle a potential major issue like this before its needed.

In section 4.3.5, you will have documented the error handling and recovery start procedures. Copy and paste the details of actual error conditions and error messages, plus a summary of recovery start procedures if applicable, into this section under the appropriate sub heading.

Depending on your actual report design, you may have a report being executed via a background batch job that then posts the results to a common Directory in SAP that the users can then retrieve from. If your design uses Directories, you will need to document the process and role responsible for archiving or clearing out these directories, so that only the most recent report(s) are held. If your design does not use Directories, then you can mark this sub heading as 'not applicable'.

Another point for consideration is who the main contacts are in the business, or per business unit, should there be a problem with the report. This will have been one of the questions you listed for your business owner when you first started writing the specification so refer back to your notes or contact the business owner again to identify these contacts. Then, should the report have a major error identified, or if it fails during batch processing, it is clear from this sub heading who must be communicated with.

Should your report have any dependencies or affiliations with other programs, you will need to make a note of those here. This will not often be applicable for reports.

Finally, list the names, roles and any authorisation checks for the business roles executing this report, as per section 4.2.4.

9.2 SAP Job Definitions

When users define a job and save it, they are actually scheduling the report. That is, specifying the job components, the steps, the start time, and the print parameters. So, to schedule a job is the same thing as to define it—a scheduled job is a job definition which has been saved.

When programs are scheduled for background processing, you are instructing the system to execute an ABAP report or an external program in the background.

It is too early in the development life cycle to actually schedule a job for your report—your functional spec hasn't even been written yet! However, from all the questions you asked and hopefully had answered when you began writing the spec, you should have a good understanding of which business units are going to use the report, how often, whether they will run it themselves on an ad hoc or regular basis, or whether the report should be scheduled to run automatically for them.

For any business units that have a requirement for the report to be run in background for them, you will need to detail any variants that will be required (i.e. per business unit's sales organisation), how often it should be run, and the printer name, if applicable, that will receive the output. From your understanding of the business requirement and the process model it fits into, you should also be able to suggest the preferred timeframe for running the report.

*   *   *TOP TIP*   *   *

Remember that a background job will perform the same tasks as if the functions were performed online. So, if a background job locks a table or updates the database, it will have an immediate result and can affect the work of online users.

*   *   *

It will ultimately be the responsibility of the deploy or implementation team (or role) in your project to ensure that the actual background jobs are scheduled and released. Your responsibility is to identify and document the need for background jobs where applicable, and to identify the elements that can be used in variants to differentiate between the same background job being run for different business units where it is not applicable to run it once for all.

9.3 Issues

By this point in the functional spec, most if not all of your initial questions on who, why, when, what and how will have been answered. Your design will have been flushed out and documented logically and clearly in section 5, and any remaining assumptions will be listed in section 4.4 Assumptions and Exclusions for every recipient of your spec to see.

If there are still any outstanding questions or issues that your project management have agreed to resolve at a later point, then they would need to be listed here to highlight them to the implementation team and act as a prompt for them to find out the status and resulting impact, before implementation.

9.4 Cross Reference Documents

When you requested all the background information to this new requirement, you may have been sent to an original Terms of Requirement document, a Blueprint Design document, or maybe just a Change Request or an Issues Log. By now, you will have documented these into section 4.1.2 Reference Documents and so can copy and paste the same information into here.

*   *   *TOP TIP*   *   *

If you have had to embed the reference documents into Section 4, then do not repeat that in this section for fear of making this spec too large to open! If this is the case, then clearly refer to the embedded documents in Section 4 and list the document names here that the Implementation Team should be interested in.

*   *   *

Chapter Seventeen

Appendices

The appendix should cover any essential information not already covered in the sections above, such as the detailed testing plan.

Note, Appendices C, D, E and F are usually completed by the Technical Team as part of their internal code reviews and handover so I won't be covering them in this book.

Appendix A: Testing Plan

We looked at why unit testing is important and what the consultant's responsibilities are in Chapter 13 on Testing Requirements. In that section, you documented the key aspects for each sub section of your report that must be successfully tested before allowing the report to move through to other testing environments.

Here in the appendix of your spec, you will need to create a Test Plan for each sub section, and then within each test plan, build the key aspects from Chapter 13 into actual test cases **to prove that the functionality works as per your design**.

FIG. 7 A Test Plan example

N o.	Test Conditions and Cases	Test Data	Expected Results	Actual Results	Pass/Fail
1	Selection Screen				
A	Verify Report can be executed using selection data in all but one mandatory field	Populate all other selection fields except the first mandatory field (use sales orgn A101, company code A100, plant Z120, date range today plus 7 days, radial not selected).Repeat for each mandatory field	All mandatory fields generate error messages when not populated with valid entries		
B	Verify Radial button can be selected to restrict report to current month's data only	use sales orgn A101, company code A100, plant Z120, date range one month ago plus 37 days, radial selected.	Report executed. Radial button selected. Data returned for current month only		
...					
2	Report Execution and Layout				
...					
3	Report Content				
...					
4	Custom Tables				
5	Authorisations				
...					

Formatting your test plan:

A test case is usually a single step, or occasionally a sequence of steps, to test the correct behavior, functionalities, and features of the report. Actual results should capture screenshots and save files as necessary to prove the requirements were met.

The following is a list of the information that may be included in a test plan:

- Test case ID

- Test case description

- Test step or order of execution number

- Related requirement(s)

- Test category

- Author

- Check boxes for whether the test is automatable and has been automated.

- Expected Result and Actual Result.

- Additional fields that may be included and completed when the tests are executed:

- Pass/fail

- Remarks

Larger test cases may also contain prerequisite states or steps, and descriptions. I like to keep my test plan format fairly simple as per the example previously shown and also included in my template.

As you write your test cases, double check to make sure that every key aspect that you have listed as a test requirement in Section 6 of your functional spec has been included in at least one test case.

Besides a description of the functionality to be tested, and the preparation required to ensure that the test can be conducted, the most time consuming part in the test case is creating the tests and modifying them when the system changes.

Appendix B: Text Elements

As part of your detailed design, you may have included requirements for the various text elements in your report (selection screen field names, report header, column headings and so on) to differ for different report users. Examples of when this might happen are when legal requirements need the report headings to be different for each company code, or when the user defined language differs from the default and the report headings need to be retrieved in that language.

Should your report have text element requirements such as these, you would need to clearly define the requirements in Section 5 of your functional spec with regards to what, how, when and where the text elements should be used. Then, rather than cluttering up your detailed design section or expecting the developer to code extensive logic to make sure he puts the correct text element in the report, refer to Appendix B for details of the actual text elements and variants.

For instance, let's consider the following scenario:

> The Report Heading needs to differ between users based on company code.

> Solution:

> Define a standard text element with an appropriate text name (e.g. Zreport_head_nnnn where nnnn is the company code). You can create standard text elements for use in your report using the standard SAPscript text processing function (transaction SO10).

The developer knows from your section 5 detailed design to populate the Report Heading with the text retrieved from this standard text element for the company code of the report.

Another aspect to text elements that may be applicable to your report is the use of text types within the data that your report is producing. For instance, an Outbound Delivery header text called 'Logistics Contact' may need to be output in the report. The text types may be document based such as this example, master data, or static (that is, the same for every report such as terms and conditions). If your report design contains these types of text elements, it is a good idea to summarise these in this section also, so as to avoid misunderstandings or confusion.

My template uses the following table to summarise all of the text element requirements in my report.

FIG. 7B Text Elements

Text Object Text ID	Text type	Report Locn	Lang	Text Value	Restrictive Criteria (please specify)

These are explained a bit more fully below:

Text Object, Text ID:

If your text elements are from documents or master data, you will need to populate this field with the SAP table object related to the text field and its configured text type. For example VBBK Z900 or LIKP Z102.

If your text element is a standard text, then put the intended text name from transaction SO10 here. For example, Zreport_head_nnnn

If your text is static, give it an identifier in case there is more than one within your report. For example 'Terms' for terms and conditions, 'Privacy' for a privacy statement

Text type:

The choices here would be:

Document (i.e. Sales Order, Delivery)

Master Data (i.e. Customer)

Static (i.e. Information that is the same for every form that is not part of the title, column headings, or a label for a given piece of data—Example: Privacy statement at the footer of the report)

Standard Text (defined in SO10)

Report Location:

The choices here would be:

HD   —Header;

IT   —Item;

FT   —Footer;

Lang:

The language that the text element is to be printed in. For example, FR for French, EN for English

Text Value:

Where possible, put the actual text value (if it is a standard text element or static text), or expected examples if it is a document or master data text type. If I have many entries or the text values are too long to fit into this small table field, then I refer to an Excel spreadsheet and then embed that document just underneath the table.

Restrictive Criteria:

Any specific exceptions, rules or special situations that could occur can be added here.

Example: Only print the Terms of Conditions when the company code language is English.

Finally, don't forget that if text elements are not relevant for your report, then mark this section as 'not applicable'.

As mentioned at the start of this section, the next four appendices are not your responsibility. They will be completed by the technical team once your functional spec has been signed off and handed over to them.

Appendix C: TS Check List

Appendix D: EPC and Code Inspector

Appendix E: QA Check List And Review Log

Appendix F: Object List

Now let's go and have a look at some good examples for each section of our functional specification.

PART 3

Examples

Website templates

Here is a reminder again of the website where you can register and download copies of both the full Report Functional spec, and the Basic Functional spec:

WWW.SAPGUIDE.CO.UK/Templates

Remember when you download the Word documents that the tips and reminders for each part of it are in 'hidden text'. To show or hide this hidden text appropriately, click on the 'paragraph' icon

Figure 8A shows an example of hidden text. Although in your template, the hidden text will show in blue not grey like here, you can tell the 'hidden text' which is in slightly larger font than the 'normal' text.

FIG. 8 A Example of hidden text used in Functional Spec template

¶

¶

This section is usually used after the development is in place for listing change requests or issues that have resulted in a change to the design. It may also be used during development if the proposed design is not appropriate, for instance, performance issues have arisen during testing or emails of the report cannot be triggered in the method described ¶

The·technical·issue·and·its·reference·number·should·be·briefly· described·and·the·resolution·documented·in·this·section.··Then·the·

* * * *TOP TIP* * * *

All your text in the functional spec will need to be written against the 'black' paragraph marks! If you accidentally type against a 'blue' paragraph mark, when you toggle to hide the hidden text, your writing will disappear also!

* * *

Good examples and why

In this part of the book, I will go through each of the main sections from the functional spec template and provide you with what I consider 'good examples'. If it is not obvious why, I will point out what I think makes it so good.

Note:

- The examples are not all from the same report!

- All examples are shown in **bold italics**, or as figures. All comments on examples are in standard text.

- All of the numbering will match the relevant sections and sub sections in the functional spec template.

3. Overview

A replacement for the legacy report (LOG_EU_ DAILY) is needed for the central logistics business to identify transportation shipments containing outbound deliveries for destinations in Europe, by freight forwarder assigned to the shipment header.

The report will be run on a daily basis to identify shipments that are of Scheduled status, where one or more of the assigned deliveries has a shipping address within the European Union. The report will contain freight, packaging, and intrastat information not available via standard SAP reports. The output of the report will need to be in a format downloadable to Excel, printable, and able to be sent as an email attachment directly from executing the report.

The central logistics team will forward this report to the freight forwarder as a booking trigger, so that an appropriate vehicle can be reserved and sent the following day for loading, and the freight forwarder has the time required to prepare the documentation to accompany the vehicle.

An interface to the freight forwarder systems has been considered and rejected at this point as too costly and not achievable within the project timelines. The volume of shipments to Europe exceeds 100 per day so it is not feasible to provide the information required by the freight forwarders manually.

This Overview clearly and briefly covers all the important questions of who, what, when, where and why the report is needed. It is at the right level of detail for an overview, as the reader of the functional spec gets a good idea of what the report is and knows that they can get further detail in other sections of the spec if need be.

4.1 General Information

4.1.1 Business Units Impacted

Central logistics, within the Supply Chain Management section have identified the requirement for this report. The Sales and Finance business units will need involvement to ensure that the freight contractual and intrastat information is included correctly.

4.1.2 Reference Documents

Business blueprint document, file name BBD_ LOG_112.doc is located in the intranet library under Central Logistics > Blueprint.

The Terms of Reference, file name TOR_LOG_REL3. doc is located in the intranet library under Central Logistics > TOR

The above examples again clearly show how to locate relevant documents and which business units should be considered not only from a design point of view, but to ensure an integrated process is in place and tested to guarantee that the new report has all the data it requires.

4.1.3 Model / Process

As it is a legal requirement for the printed customer invoice to show both the pre-printed delivery number and the SAP delivery number, the scheduler/dispatcher must ensure that all pre-printed delivery numbers are scanned or manually entered into the custom control table every day. The report is run at the end of the day, prior to billing processes, and those deliveries that have been missed or not entered in the table on a given day are filtered. Subsequently, the user contacts the haulier to get the barcode number and then updates the custom table manually. This process is represented as shown:

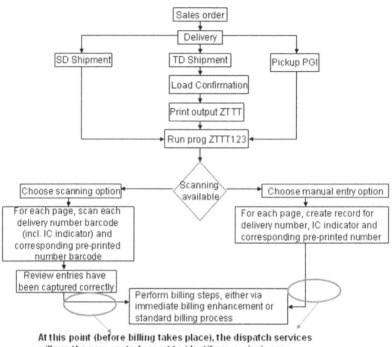

FIG 9A – 'Good' Process Flow example

Okay, now I am not saying that this process flow is the very best, but it meets the standard that I would expect because it clearly shows where this new report fits into the existing business process. You can see the preceding steps in the flow, and also what other custom development is part of the same process. That will help identifying dependencies, and understanding integration testing.

4.1.4 Scope

All Bulk and Packed Outbound Shipments for Company code ZTTT, containing Fuels and Lubes products. Pickup Shipments are also within scope.

4.2 Controls

4.2.1 Report Description

It is a legal requirement that all customer invoices generated from company code ZTTT show both the pre-printed delivery number and the SAP delivery number. To ensure that the pre-printed delivery number has been captured prior to billing, the report will be run on a daily basis and will be used for all deliveries originating from company code ZTTT plants. This will cover bulk and packed pickups and shipments, for both fuels and lubes products. As the report will only ever be run by authorised roles in the foreground, background jobs will not be required.

A selection screen will allow the user to select whether to view all shipments that have dispatched that day, or only those that have not been scanned and do not yet have an entry in the ZTTT_LINKT custom table. The user will only be able to run the report on a 24-hour basis (i.e. Monday to Tuesday or Thursday to Friday) to avoid any performance issues of collecting large amounts of data.

The starting point for the report will be transaction /ZTTT_MISLINKT. Mandatory entries in the selection screen will be the Shipping Point, Dispatch Start date and time, Dispatch End date and time. The options for Transportation Group and Deliveries are represented by radio buttons. For the transportation group, we can have the option of Packed, Bulk or both included. For deliveries, we have the option of choosing between those that are not scanned and / or all the deliveries that are scanned and not scanned.

A second custom table (ZTTT_ EXCLNOPLN) is required to contain entries of the notional plants which are not to be treated as intercompany, as they will only print one delivery note. This second custom table will resolve the issue of an intercompany delivery which has two entries in table ZTTT_LINKT, one for the customer delivery note and another for the intercompany delivery note. If any of the intercompany deliveries are not mapped into the table, this will show up in the report as an un-recorded pre-printed number. If for an intercompany delivery, the notional plant is present in the table ZTTT_EXCLNOPLN, this will be treated as a normal delivery. That is, a normal delivery only has one delivery note.

Report functionality

- *It is possible to refresh the results of the report (e.g. after the user has updated some missing numbers)*

- *It is possible to export the report to Excel*

- *It is possible to email the report*

- *It is possible to sort the columns*

Performance

- *Multiple users running the report at the same time for the same set of data*

- *Multiple users running the report at the same time for a different set of data*

This example of a Report Description is quite long but it needs to be to cover what the report will produce in detail, how it is executed, how often, the methods of output, starting point, mandatory fields in selection, and the use of custom tables. All in short, understandable sentences!

4.2.2 Report Controls

This report is restricted to users within the company code ZTTT. The data within the report is not confidential, however only business role LOG123 will have a requirement to run the report.

4.2.3 Dependencies

This report has dependencies on a form for company code ZTTT produced at TD shipment load confirmation. The output is ZTTT and the RIEF reference is LOGF042.

There is also a dependency on the enhancement for pre-printed numbers, program ZTTT123. This RIEF reference is LOGE039.

In the dependency section, it is not necessary to describe the other developments in detail. You just need to highlight any interdependencies with any other developments, either in progress, planned or already in existence.

4.2.4 Access Restrictions

The report is restricted to the authorisation object company code. Only users authorised for company code ZTTT may access the report. Within this company code, only role LOG123 has a requirement

to run the report. The transaction code will be /
ZTTT_MISLINKT

Remembering back to Part 2 of the book, it is not important
to detail the actual authorisation object if you are unsure what
it is as a clearly worded description such as this one will do
fine.

4.3 Processing

4.3.1 Starting Conditions

*The form ZTTT should have been successfully
printed and the pre-printed number on the form
scanned into the custom table ZTTT_LINKT. After
this point in the business process and before Billing
begins, the report should be run using transaction /
ZTTT_MISLINKT.*

4.3.2 Frequency

*The report will be run daily, towards the end of each
main shift. Shift 1 ends at 14:00 WST and Shift 2 at
22:00 WST. It is likely that more than one user may
run the report at the same time.*

4.3.3 Volume

*Daily number of deliveries for lubes including bulk/
packed/pick-ups is approximately 180-200.*

*Daily number of shipments and pickups for fuels is
approximately 780.*

4.3.4 Archiving

It is expected that the entries in the custom table ZTTT_LINKT will build up over time and may cause performance issues in future. The business has agreed that only the past three months of data is required in the table, all other earlier entries can be deleted. The preferred method for archiving these earlier entries is still under debate. Refer to Business Issue reference LOG23.

4.3.5 Error Handling and Recovery Restart

When the report is run in foreground by the user, the appropriate error messages should display in the language of the user. Refer to Section 5.4.2 for further details.

4.4 Assumptions and Exclusions

- *The number of pages in the outbound delivery output ZTTT will not be taken into consideration. If at least one page from the delivery has been scanned, then the system will assume that all other pages have been scanned also. Therefore the delivery will not show on the "not yet scanned" report.*

- *For intercompany deliveries, a customer delivery note (11th digit of barcode = 0) and an intercompany delivery note (11th digit of barcode = 1) are printed. If either one, or both of these are missing from the custom table ZTTT_LINKT then the system will need to pull this through into the report as having an unrecorded pre-printed number*

- *Business Issue reference LOG23 regarding method of archiving entries older than three months from custom table ZTTT_LINKT will be resolved prior to Acceptance Testing.*

5.1 Distribution

The report may be printed or downloaded/ exported to an Excel spreadsheet, which can then be subsequently forwarded to other authorized users via e-mail (where this is legally/fiscally allowed).

5.2 Transaction Code

The transaction code for the new report will be / ZTTT_MISLINKT

5.3 Selection Screen

5.3.1 Criteria

The selection criteria for this report will be grouped into three section headings to make it clearer for the users—data, transportation group and deliveries.

Data

- *Shipping Point: This is mandatory and entered by the user. The system should allow multiple shipping points to be entered*

- *Dispatch Start Date: Defaulted as 24 hrs earlier at the point of execution of report.*

- *Dispatch Start Time: Defaulted as 24 hrs earlier at the point of execution of report.*

- *Dispatch End Date: Defaulted as 24 hrs earlier at the point of execution of report.*

- *Dispatch End Time: Defaulted as 24 hrs earlier at the point of execution of report.*

Transportation Group

- *Bulk: This is a radial button. If selected, should limit selection to only those transportation groups defined for bulk lubes and fuels products. That is, all transportation groups other than 0001.*

- *Packed: This is a radial button. If selected, should limit selection to only those transportation groups defined for packed lubes products. That is, transportation group 0001.*

- *All: This radial button will select all Bulk, fuels and packed Transportation Groups in the selection criteria. This is the default option.*

Deliveries

- *Not Yet Scanned: This radial button will pick only those deliveries that are not yet scanned.*

- *All: This radio button will select all the deliveries (scanned and not-scanned) present in the system. This is the default option. All the deliveries that do not have a preprinted number will be highlighted in red. Those where pre-printed number is already maintained should be shown in normal font/color.*

Note: The system will automatically default the dispatch end date and time to current date/time and the start date and time as 24 hours earlier but the user will be able to choose the desired 24-hour period. Use the user's time zone and not that of the system. The user has an option of overriding the Start/End date and time, provided they are within a 24 hour window.

Please upload the following text behind the Info button on the selection screen to provide onscreen help to users:

Background

It is a legal requirement that all customer invoices generated from company code ZTTT show both the pre-printed delivery number and the SAP delivery number. To ensure that the pre-printed delivery number has been captured prior to billing, this report will be run on a daily basis by the Logistics Scheduler role (LOG123) in company code ZTTT. It will be used for all deliveries originating from company code ZTTT plants, including bulk and packed pickups and shipments, for both fuels and lubes products. The report will identify all deliveries that have not yet had the pre-printed delivery number scanned into custom table ZTTT_LINKT, which is a required step before billing of those deliveries can take place.

Report Description

A selection screen will allow the user to select whether to view all shipments that have been dispatched that day, or only those that have not been scanned and do not yet have an entry in the ZTTT_LINKT custom table. The user will only be able to run the report on a 24-hour basis (i.e. Monday to Tuesday or Thursday to Friday) to avoid any performance issues of collecting large amounts of data. Shipping point and dispatch date and time are mandatory fields.

The report output can be viewed on screen in ALV format, downloaded to Excel or sent as a PDF document via email. Depending on the selection criteria used, the report output will list all those deliveries that have not yet been scanned, including ship to and haulier details, so that the Logistics Scheduler can contact the haulier to obtain the pre-printed delivery number for manual addition to the custom table. A normal delivery only has one delivery note and therefore if this has not been scanned, it will show in the report. An intercompany delivery has two delivery notes (one customer version, one intercompany version). Unless the supplying plant is an exception noted in custom table ZTTT_EXCLNOPLN, the report will expect two pre-printed numbers to have been scanned.

Access Required

Only role LOG123 authorised for company code ZTTT will have access to this report.

This is a good example of 'Criteria' as it covers all the required points:

- The fields that are required,

- How to group them logically,

- Which are mandatory,

- Which have default values

- Which are radial buttons versus input fields

- Whether multiple entries can be used.

It also includes the summary of the report to be loaded as screen help behind the information icon on the selection screen, providing a very professional and thorough finish to this part of the specification.

5.3.2 Attributes

Short Description: Report for Pre-printed Number Maintenance

Original Language: EN (English)

Screen Type: Selection screen

Settings: Hold scroll position

FIG. 10 A Report Attributes Mock-up example

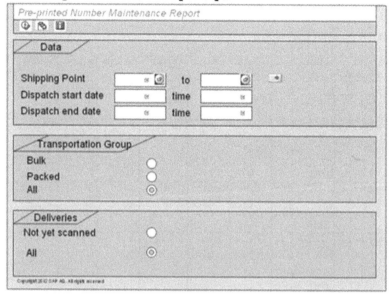

The Report Attributes in figure 10A clearly show a simple mock-up of how the selection screen will look, and provides enough detail for the technical team to proceed. Remember not to spend too much time working on the finer details of any mock-ups or screenshots as the aim is to provide clear, concise details but still get the functional spec produced and signed off on time.

5.3.3 Elements List

FIG 10B Elements List example

Field Description	Field	Check Table	Field Type	Format	Length	Mand	Default value
Data			label				
Shipping Point	VSTEL	TVST	Input	CHAR	4	Y	
Dispatch start date	WADAT_I ST LOAD_ED DTA	LIKP OIGS	Input	DATS	8	Y	24 hours prior to end date
Dispatch start time	OIWATIM LOAD_ED TMA	LIKP OIGS	Input	TIMS	6	Y	Same as end time
Dispatch end date	WADAT_I ST LOAD_ED DTA	LIKP OIGS	Input	DATS	8	Y	Users current date
Dispatch end time	OIWATIM LOAD_ED TMA	LIKP OIGS	input	TIMS	6	Y	Users current time
Transportatio n Group			label				
Bulk			Radial				
Packed			Radial				
All			Radial				
Deliveries			Label				
Not yet scanned			Radial				
All			radial				

The elements list shown in figure 10B covers all of the fields in the selection screen and in enough detail for the development team to understand the requirements. To make it even better, it could refer to comments or notes (e.g. Note 1, note 2 etc) in the default value column and then include example entries along with a more detailed description of how to determine the default values to be populated. This would be consistent with the approach that I prefer to use for the next section, detailing the extraction logic for the report itself and the actual fields in the report.

5.4 Data Extraction Criteria

FIG 10C Extraction Logic Process Flow example

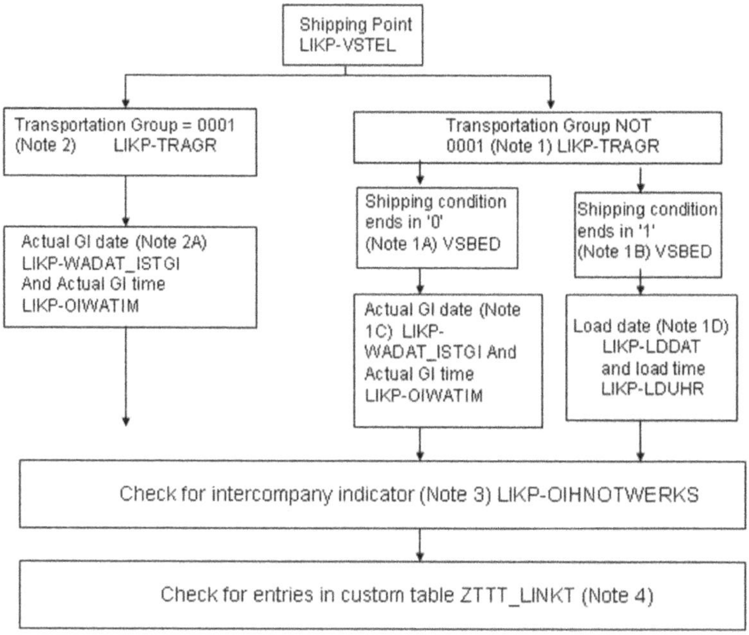

```
                        ┌─────────────────┐
                        │ Shipping Point  │
                        │ LIKP-VSTEL      │
                        └─────────────────┘
```

Transportation Group = 0001 (Note 2) LIKP-TRAGR	Transportation Group NOT 0001 (Note 1) LIKP-TRAGR

	Shipping condition ends in '0' (Note 1A) VSBED	Shipping condition ends in '1' (Note 1B) VSBED

Actual GI date (Note 2A) LIKP-WADAT_ISTGI And Actual GI time LIKP-OIWATIM	Actual GI date (Note 1C) LIKP-WADAT_ISTGI And Actual GI time LIKP-OIWATIM	Load date (Note 1D) LIKP-LDDAT and load time LIKP-LDUHR

Check for intercompany indicator (Note 3) LIKP-OIHNOTWERKS

Check for entries in custom table ZTTT_LINKT (Note 4)

I think this simple flowchart (figure 10C) is a good example because its clean, clear and links the main extraction logic to the relevant 'note' which we will see in the following 'Fields in the Report' section.

5.4.1 Fields in the Report

FIG 10D Fields in the Report example

Field Description	Field	Type	Column heading	Length	Position	Comment
Delivery number	LIKP-VBELN	CHAR	Delivery	10	1	See notes 1 and 2
Plant	LIPS-WERKS	CHAR	Plant	4	2	Use delivery number to retrieve
Shipping point	LIPS-VSTEL	CHAR	Shipping Point	4	3	Use delivery number to retrieve
Shipment number	VBFA-VBELN	CHAR	Shipment	10	4	See note 5
Pre-printed number	ZTTT_LINKT-PPNUM	CHAR	Pre-Printed Number	8	5	Use delivery number to retrieve
Creation Date	ZTTT_LINKT-CRDATE	DATS	Creation date	8	6	Use delivery number to retrieve the date it was scanned
Intercompany indicator	ZTTT_LINKT-INTERCO_IND	CHAR	Intercomp any	1	7	Use delivery number to retrieve. 1 means yes, 0 means no
Dispatch date	LIKP-WADAT_IST	DATS	Dispatch date	8	8	See notes 1 and 2
Dispatch time	LIKP-OIWATIM	TIMS	Dispatch time	6	9	See notes 1 and 2
Ship to partner	LIKP-KUNNR	CHAR	Ship To	10	10	Use delivery number to retrieve
Ship to Name	KNAI-NAME1	CHAR	Ship To Name	25	11	Use ship to party number to retrieve
Haulier	VTTK-	CHAR	Haulier	25	12	See note 6

FIG 10E Extraction Logic Notes example

Note 1 Extraction criteria for retrieving Delivery Number
Using the Shipping Point, Dispatch Start/End Date and Time and Transportation Group get all the deliveries for the dates entered in the selection criteria.

Note 1A
- If Transportation Group TRAGR is not equal to 0001 and Shipping Condition ends in "0" or (Fuel Pickups)
  - ➢ Find Actual GI Date LIKP-WADAT_IST and Actual GI Time LIKP-OIWATIM and display those deliveries that match the selection criteria entered by the user.
  - ➢ Check if LIKP-OIHNOTWERKS is populated, if populated, the system then needs to perform a check on the custom table ZTTT_EXCLNOPLN. If present, expect one entry in ZTTT_LINKT. If the plant is not present then expect two entries in ZTTT_LINKT (one for customer delivery note and one for intercompany delivery note).

Note 1B
- If Transportation Group TRAGR is not equal to 0001 and Shipping Condition ends in "1" or (Fuel Pickups)
  - ➢ Find Actual GI Date LIKP-WADAT_IST and Actual GI Time LIKP-OIWATIM and display those deliveries that match the selection criteria entered by the user.
  - ➢ Check if LIKP-OIHNOTWERKS is populated, if populated, the system then needs to perform a check on the custom table ZTTT_EXCLNOPLN. If present, expect one entry in ZTTT_LINKT. If the plant is not present then expect two entries in ZTTT_LINKT (one for customer delivery note and one for intercompany delivery note).

Note 1C
- If Transportation Group TRAGR is not equal to 0001 and Shipping Condition ends in "2" or (Aviation Fuel deliveries)
  - ➢ Find Actual GI Date LIKP-WADAT_IST and Actual GI Time LIKP-OIWATIM and display those deliveries that match the selection criteria entered by the user.

These examples of the table containing the actual fields in the report (Fig. 10D) and the extraction logic notes (Fig. 10E) that go with it, although not a complete sample, show enough for you to understand the method that I am proposing. Where the column of the report can be populated through simple logic such as 'use the delivery number to retrieve LIPS-VSTEL', then the logic is contained under the 'comments' field in the table. It is only when the logic gets more complicated, where perhaps there are conditions with varied extraction logic, that the developer is going to need more detail. That is when it is useful to refer the developer to a note below the table that will contain the full extraction criteria logic.

It is also in this section of the functional spec that any new custom tables would be defined, and the corresponding logic for using the new table and its contents would be explained. I have included an example of this in FIG 10F.

FIG 10F New Custom Table example

Custom table for Validating Notional Plant
A new custom table is required as part of the intercompany steps detailed below. This custom table will contain entries of the exception notional plants which are not to be treated as intercompany as they will only print one delivery note.

This table will be a configuration table and entries will be maintained across Clients using revtracs.

New table name: ZTTT_ EXCLNOPLN
New transaction: /ZTTT_EXCLNOPLN
Transaction type: Table maintenance

Role: – this table will be updated by the Hypercare team via revtracs across all environments, not by business users

Short Text	Field name	Field	Primary key	Typ e	Length	Exampl e
Direct sales notional plant.	Notional plant code	OIHNOTWERK S	X	A/N	4	B234

5.4.2 *Error Handling*

FIG 10G Error Handling and Error Messages example

- Appropriate error messages must be displayed for entries that are missing or invalid, either in the selection screen or when displaying the report itself.
- If no valid data can be found for any column, then the report should show a blank in that column / row.
- If the selection criteria entered returns no data at all, an error message should be shown.

Error Condition	Error message
Selection Screen	
Shipping point not entered	"Enter shipping point"
Dispatch Start date not present	"Enter dispatch start date"
Dispatch Start time not present	"Enter dispatch start time"
Dispatch End date not present	"Enter dispatch end date"
Dispatch End time not present	"Enter dispatch end time"
Plant on delivery is non-Turkish plant	"Delivery does not contain a Turkish plant"
Date range is more than 24 hours	"Date range between Start and End date should be less than 24 hours"
End date and time is greater than Start date and time.	"End date and time cannot be greater than Start date and time"
Try and save date and time fields in the Variant	"Date and time fields cannot be saved in the variant"
No data found	"No data found for the selection criteria entered"

This is a reasonable example of the error handling required for the new report in that it clearly covers the mandatory fields and main conditions. It is often a good idea to draft the error conditions like this and come back to it again after you have re-read your design section and thought more about the testing requirements that you need to cover. Doing this often flushes out even more error messages that will be required.

5.4.3 *Report Output Format*

FIG 10H Report Output Format example

Report Output Format
Report Header Information
The values displayed will include some that are present on the selection screen.
- Shipping Point
- Transportation Group
- Start Date
- End Date

Report Detail Information
This report will use the SAP standard ALV format. The same color code is to be used as it is displayed in the mock-up.

Item Details
- Delivery
- Plant
- Shipping Point
- Shipment
- Pre-Printed Number
- Creation Date
- Intercompany Indicator
- Dispatch Date
- Dispatch Time
- Ship-to party
- Ship to Name
- Haulier Reference
- Haulier Reference 2
- Haulier number
- Haulier Name
- Haulier Phone

An example and corresponding mockup of the report is shown as below

Mockup_example.xls

In this section, it is important to explain any additional formatting requirements such as report headers and footers, page break requirements, page numbering and so on. It is a very good idea to include a simple mock-up of how the actual report output will look so that it takes some of the guess work out of the development for the technical team. It is also a good idea to double-check that your list of items to appear in the rows of the report include ALL of the fields that you have in your mock-up and that you have provided extraction logic for!

5.4.4 Sort Sequence

Sorting Sequence.

- ***Delivery, Plant, Shipping point and Shipment.**
  These should be sorted in ascending order.*

- ***Pre-printed Number**
  These are sorted in ascending order with letters having higher priority than numbers.*

- ***This should be sorted in ascending order***

- ***Intercompany Indicator**
  This should be sorted either as 0 (non intercompany delivery) or 1 (intercompany deliveries).*

- ***Ship-To**
  These are sorted according to Customer Number, with letters having higher priority than numbers.*

- ***Haulier Number**
  This should be sorted in ascending order.*

This example is sufficient to let the development team know the requirements for displaying the report output. Remember that if you do not document it, the decision will be made for you and may not be as per the end user's expectations.

Section 6 Testing Requirements

6.1 Selection Screen

- *Layout of selection screen is as per detailed design in section 5 of this spec*

- *Radial buttons can be activated*

- *Multiple values can be entered for every input field*

- *Default values are correct for the user's timezone*

- *Date and time dispatch start to end fields cannot be shorter than a 24 hour period*

- *After executing and returning to the selection screen, date and time defaults have refreshed to current values*

- *Invalid field entries are not accepted*

- *Mandatory fields cannot be left empty*

- *Optional fields can be left empty*

- *Selection screen variants can be created, retrieved and changed*

- *All error messages for the selection screen are triggered appropriately and accurately*

The above list of test requirements adequately covers all the aspects of the selection screen that need to be tested, including positive and negative tests. As long as all of these are included in at least one test case each, the selection screen should be thoroughly unit tested.

6.2 Report Execution and Layout

- *Report can be executed to screen*

- *Report can be printed to a specified Laser printer*

- *Report can be downloaded to an Excel file*

- *Report can be sent by email*

- *Only valid external email addresses can be used*

- *Email subject line is as per detailed design requirements*

- *Attachment in the email is 'read only'*

- *Attachment in the email can be opened without error*

- *Attachment in the email is in the correct layout*

- *Printed output is in landscape format*

- *Report header is accurately shown when executed to screen, downloaded to Excel and emailed*

- *Report items are in the order specified in the detail design*

- *Column data is sorted according to the sequence specified in detail design*

- *All standard ALV functionality is available and working correctly*

- *Layout is correct when report is a single page output*

- *Layout is correct when report covers multiple pages*

The above example appears to thoroughly test each of the required execution methods and all of the layout requirements specified. The only way to ensure that your own test requirements list is complete, is to go back through your detailed design, line by line, and make sure that every requirement you have asked for is included in the appropriate test requirements sub section.

6.3 Report Content

- *Packed lubes deliveries, same shipping point, not yet scanned show correctly*

- *Packed lubes deliveries, same shipping point, already scanned show only when All is selected*

- *Packed lubes IC deliveries, same shipping point, not yet scanned show correctly*

- *Packed lubes IC deliveries, same shipping point, already scanned show only when All is selected*

- *Packed lubes pickups, same shipping point, not yet scanned show correctly*

- *Packed lubes pickups, same shipping point, already scanned show only when All is selected*

- *Bulk lubes deliveries, same shipping point, not yet scanned show correctly*

- *Bulk lubes deliveries, same shipping point, already scanned show only when All is selected*

- *Bulk lubes IC deliveries, same shipping point, not yet scanned show correctly*

- *Bulk lubes IC deliveries, same shipping point, already scanned show only when All is selected*

- *Bulk lubes pickups, same shipping point, not yet scanned show correctly*

- *Bulk lubes pickups, same shipping point, already scanned show only when All is selected*

- *Bulk lubes IC deliveries where plant is in exclusion table, not yet scanned, shows only one missing pre-printed number*

- *Bulk lubes IC deliveries where plant is in exclusion table, already scanned, shows one pre-printed number, none not yet scanned, when All is selected*

- *Bulk lubes IC pickups where plant is in exclusion table, not yet scanned, shows only one missing pre-printed number*

- *Bulk lubes IC pickups where plant is in exclusion table, already scanned, shows one pre-printed number, none not yet scanned, when All is selected*

- *Bulk lubes IC STO where plant is in exclusion table, not yet scanned, shows only one missing pre-printed number*

- *Bulk lubes IC STO where plant is in exclusion table, already scanned, shows one pre-printed number, none not yet scanned, when All is selected*

- *Bulk fuels pickups, same shipping point, not yet scanned show correctly*

- *Bulk fuels pickups, same shipping point, already scanned show only when All is selected*

- ***Report contents are accurate when multiple shipping points are used in the selection***

- ***Report contents are accurate when deliveries at different load statuses are included***

- ***Report contents are accurate when deliveries at different goods issue status are included***

- ***Report contents are accurate when multi page deliveries are included***

I have chosen this example to show just how long and detailed these test requirements can be. In this example, the consultant has listed a separate test requirement for each combination of product type and delivery type, to ensure that she does not miss any when she goes to create her test cases. Whether you choose to break the test requirements down like this, or to group them by product type or other relevant criteria, the important part is to make sure that you have thought through the different types of data that the report will use, and how the contents of the report may differ accordingly. If different test data criteria (for instance, delivery types) will result in the same report content, then it may be possible for you to summarise the testing of them into one test requirement. Your test case would then need to use each of the different delivery types in its test data to prove the requirement has been met.

6.4 Custom Tables

Custom table ZTTT_EXCLNOPLAN

- ***Transaction code brings up the table for maintenance***

- *New entries can be created in the table*

- *Table entries can be changed*

- *Table entries can be deleted*

- *Table entries can be displayed*

- *Only valid table entries can be saved*

- *All entries must be unique*

- *Table entries are accurately retrieved and reported*

This example is fairly self explanatory. Any custom tables built for your report need to be thoroughly tested in their own right. The test requirement for whether the table entries are actually used correctly by the report can be included in the report content test cases.

6.5 Authorisations

Report transaction /ZTTT_MISLINKT

- *Only users authorised assigned role LOG123 with company code ZTTT should be able to execute this report*

- *Authorised users can execute the report to screen, print and email the output*

- *Unauthorised users in company codes other than ZTTT cannot access the report*

- ***Users authorised for company code ZTTT but not assigned to role LOG123 cannot access the report***

This example covers the basics needed in authorisation testing, including negative tests. The consultant needs to understand the concepts involved in authorisation testing and cover these in the test requirements.

6.6 Test Data

Use transaction VL06O Outbound Delivery Monitor to identify deliveries and then drill into each to filter as follows:

Packed lubes deliveries—transportation group 0001

Packed lubes pickups—shipping condition ends in '1'

Packed lubes IC—delivery header IC indicator set

Bulk lubes deliveries—transportation group not 0002

Bulk lubes pickups—shipping condition ends in '1'

Bulk lubes IC—delivery header IC indicator set

Bulk fuels deliveries—transportation group 0003 or 0004

Shipping points for company code ZTTT—T100 to T124

I have not put the full content of this example in due to size constraints but it goes on to describe how to identify and check test data for all of the report content requirements previously listed. Rather than providing an actual spreadsheet of delivery and shipment numbers, the consultant has taken a more forward thinking approach and described how to find the data. This means that the technical team, the actual tester, and other teams wanting to understand the report in future can all find their own data, rather than relying solely on the consultant to come up with the data for them each time they have a need to test.

6.7 Other Test Cycles

The following Acceptance and Integration Testing scenarios for company code ZTTT will need to be amended to include this new report:

- *Packed lubes deliveries*

- *Bulk lubes deliveries*

- *Bulk fuels deliveries*

- *Bulk lubes IC deliveries*

- *Packed lubes IC deliveries*

- *Bulk lubes IC STO deliveries*

- *Pickup scenarios for packed and bulk lubes and Fuels*

Ideally, the actual test scenario names and location (i.e. intranet, testing database etc) should be included but as a minimum, listing the business process scenarios that will be impacted by the new report such as this example is sufficient.

7. Issues

7.1 Technical Issue 173 re Performance

Background

During Acceptance Testing in environment A94, users complained that the report was taking over ten minutes to run, regardless of the selection criteria used. Subsequent investigations by the Technical team have found that the Select statements on some of the tables are hampered by the volume of data in those tables. Tech issue 173 raised to cover defects 112, 115 and 117.

Resolution

The following changes will be made to address the performance issue:

- *Transactional date range will be a mandatory selection criteria. Refer to updated sections 4.3.3 Volume of Data, 5.3.1 Criteria, 5.3.3 Elements List*

- *A validation check will be included to ensure the date range entered does not exceed 31 days. Refer to updated sections 5.4.2 Error Handling and section 8 Tech spec*

- *Select statements on the LIKP and LIPS tables will be reviewed Refer to updated section 8 Tech spec*

This is the same example I used in Part Two of the book to explain how to complete this section of the spec if changes are made after the spec has been signed off. It clearly states the reason for the update and the areas of the functional spec that now reflect changes as a result. Although it is not a section you will have to complete when you initially draft your functional spec, it is a good idea to be familiar with a professional, standardised method of updating the spec should the need arise.

9. Implementation and Deploy

9.1 User Instructions

- *Prior to implementation, maintain table ZTTT_ EXCLNOPLN with plants that are to be excluded from Intercompany update to the custom table ZTTT _LINKT.*

- *A normal intercompany delivery will have two entries (customer delivery note and intercompany delivery note) to be scanned to the ZTTT_LINKT table. If the plant present on the delivery is included in the ZTTT_ EXCLNOPLN table, this delivery should be treated as a normal delivery with only one entry in the ZTTT_LINKT table. If an entry is missing in table ZTTT_EXCLNOPLN, the delivery will be processed as though an intercompany delivery.*

9.1.1 Procedures for Processing

- *Enter the transaction /ZTTT_MISLINKT and fill in the selection criteria*

- *When entering the selection criteria*

  ➤ *Shipping points to include only those from company code ZTTT and not from other countries or third party plants.*

  ➤ *Dispatch End Date and time will be the current User time.*

  ➤ *Choose the Transportation group for bulk, Packed or both.*

  ➤ *Choose the radial button to display all deliveries or only those deliveries that are not yet scanned.*

Note: The Dispatch start/end date and time can be manually changed, however, the date/time range must be within or equal to a 24 hour window.

- *Press execute or F8 to run the report.*

- *It is possible to*

  ➤ *Refresh the content of the report.*

  ➤ *Export the content of the report.*

  ➤ *Sort the contents of the report.*

  ➤ *Email the report.*

9.1.2 Frequency

The report will be run daily, towards the end of each main shift. Shift 1 ends at 14:00 WST and Shift 2 at 22:00 WST. It is likely that more than one user may run the report at the same time.

9.1.3 Manual Processing

If the SAP system is down completely, it is recommended that a manual process of recording the pre-printed delivery numbers physically issued is used until the system can be updated with the deliveries and manual entries made into the custom table ZTTT_LINKT.

If the SAP system is available but this report is not, then users would need to manually check that each physical delivery has an entry in table ZTTT_LINKT. Table browse transaction SE16N could be used by an authorised user for this purpose until the report is available again.

9.1.4 Error Handling

When the report is run in foreground by the user, the appropriate error messages should display in the language of the user.

FIG 10G Error Handling and Error Messages example

- Appropriate error messages must be displayed for entries that are missing or invalid, either in the selection screen or when displaying the report itself.
- If no valid data can be found for any column, then the report should show a blank in that column / row.
- If the selection criteria entered returns no data at all, an error message should be shown.

Error Condition	Error message
Selection Screen	
Shipping point not entered	"Enter shipping point"
Dispatch Start date not present	"Enter dispatch start date"
Dispatch Start time not present	"Enter dispatch start time"
Dispatch End date not present	"Enter dispatch end date"
Dispatch End time not present	"Enter dispatch end time"
Plant on delivery is non-Turkish plant	"Delivery does not contain a Turkish plant"
Date range is more than 24 hours	"Date range between Start and End date should be less than 24 hours"
End date and time is greater than Start date and time.	"End date and time cannot be greater than Start date and time"
Try and save date and time fields in the Variant	"Date and time fields cannot be saved in the variant"
No data found	"No data found for the selection criteria entered"

9.1.5 Clearing Out Directories

No directories are used with this report. The users run the report twice daily, in foreground. If the output is downloaded to Excel, the file is stored locally on the user's shared directory.

9.1.6 Problem Reporting

This report is specific to company code ZTTT. If there are problems with the report or its availability, appropriate management for the logistics business within this company code should be advised, along with any users assigned to role LOG123.

9.1.7 SAP Programs and Related Documents

This report has dependencies on a form for company code ZTTT produced at TD shipment load confirmation. The output is ZTTT and the RIEF reference is LOGF042.

There is also a dependency on the enhancement for pre-printed numbers, program ZTTT123. This RIEF reference is LOGE039.

9.1.8 Security Checks

The report is restricted to the authorisation object company code. Only users authorised for company code ZTTT may access the report. Within this company code, only role LOG123 has a requirement to run the report. The transaction code will be / ZTTT_MISLINKT

9.2 SAP Job Definitions

No SAP job definitions are required for the implementation of this report.

9.3 Issues

As at the time of drafting this functional spec, an outstanding business issue remained regarding how the custom table ZTTT_LINKT entries would be archived. Please check prior to implementation that the issue was resolved.

Business Issue reference LOG23 regarding method of archiving entries older than three months from

custom table ZTTT_LINKT will be resolved prior to Acceptance Testing.

9.4 Cross Reference Documents

Business blueprint document, file name BBD_ LOG_112.doc is located in the intranet library under Central Logistics > Blueprint.

The Terms of Reference, file name TOR_LOG_REL3. doc is located in the intranet library under Central Logistics > TOR

The examples I have shown for the Implementation section all come from the same report functional spec. You can see how it is providing the implementation team with clear, easy to follow details on how the report is used, by whom and when. Putting all this information together, even though some of the sub sections are repeating information from other parts of the functional spec, is allowing the implementation team to get this overview of the report without having to flick back and forth within your functional spec, saving them time and effort so that they can concentrate on the tasks they need to do in making sure your report successfully goes live.

Appendix A Testing Plan

FIG 11A Test Plan Example

No.	Test Conditions and Cases	Test Data	Expected Results	Actual Results	Pass/Fail
1	Selection Screen				
A	Verify layout of selection screen is as per detailed design; radial buttons can be selected and default date and time are valid for the user executing the report	User id TEST1 has WST time zone	Layout is as per design. Radial buttons can be selected. Date and time defaults are correct for WST time zone		
B	Verify report cannot be executed without valid entries in all mandatory fields	Shipping points T100 to T124 User id TEST1 with WST time zone	Shipping point, dispatch date and time are all mandatory. Invalid entries generate error message on execution. Dispatch start to end period cannot be less than 24 hours.		
C	Verify selection criteria can be saved in variant	Shipping points T100-!124 User id TEST1 with WST time zone	Multiple shipping points can be entered. Variant can be saved and retrieved		
2	Report Execution and Layout				
A	Verify execution to screen produces correct	Shipping points T100-!124	Executed to screen ok, ALV format produced		

This partial test plan example (Fig. 11A) shows the consultant bringing together the test requirements into test cases. It is not necessary to create a test case per test requirement, as long as you can verify that every test requirement is included in at least one test case. Basic test data is given, along with expected results. I have found that using a table in a word document such as this can be a bit limiting with regards to detail. Occasionally I have found that embedding an Excel spreadsheet with full details of the test plan including test steps and detailed expected results works better. Often, you will be asked to document your test plans into a specific test management tool such as Test Director or QaTraq so it is sufficient to include the test cases at the level of detail shown in Fig 11A in the functional spec, and then go to a lower level of detail in the actual test management tool which may have a number of mandatory fields and sections to be completed.

Appendix B Text Elements

FIG 12A Text Element example

Text Object Text ID	Text type	Report Locn	Lang	Text Value	Restrictive Criteria (please specify)
LIKP Z102	Doc	Item	En	Logistics controller ph 5551213 extn 7235	If delivery has partner function ZA, retrieve this text
ZHEAD _S122	Std text	Footer	ES	Los productos que se vuelve	Where sales organisation is S102, retrieve this statement

Figure 12A gives an example of two different types of text element used in the same report. This appendix is of particular use to summarise when there are many different text elements, perhaps with different languages and restrictive criteria.

This brings us to the end of this guide to writing a report functional specification. I hope that you are able to take many positive tips and best practices to apply in your every day role of functional consultant.

Strive to be the best and stand out as a professional, knowledgeable, productive consultant.

DISCLAIMER

This publication contains references to the products of SAP AG. SAP, R/3, SAP NetWeaver, Duet, PartnerEdge, ByDesign, SAP BusinessObjects Explorer, StreamWork, and other SAP products and services mentioned herein as well as their respective logos are trademarks or registered trademarks of SAP AG in Germany and other countries.

Business Objects and the Business Objects logo, BusinessObjects, Crystal Reports, Crystal Decisions, Web Intelligence, Xcelsius, and other Business Objects products and services mentioned herein as well as their respective logos are trademarks or registered trademarks of Business Objects Software Ltd. Business Objects is an SAP company.

Sybase and Adaptive Server, iAnywhere, Sybase 365, SQL Anywhere, and other Sybase products and services mentioned herein as well as their respective logos are trademarks or registered trademarks of Sybase, Inc. Sybase is an SAP company.

SAP AG is neither the author nor the publisher of this publication and is not responsible for its content. SAP Group shall not be liable for errors or omissions with respect to the materials. The only warranties for SAP Group products and services are those that are set forth in the express warranty statements accompanying such products and services, if any. Nothing herein should be construed as constituting an additional warranty.